The Object Lessons series achieves something very close to magic: the books take ordinary—even banal—objects and animate them with a rich history of invention, political struggle, science, and popular mythology. Filled with fascinating details and conveyed in sharp, accessible prose, the books make the everyday world come to life. Be warned: once you've read a few of these, you'll start walking around your house, picking up random objects, and musing aloud: 'I wonder what the story is behind this thing?'

Steven Johnson, author of *Where Good Ideas Come From* and *How We Got to Now*

In 1957 the French critic and semiotician Roland Barthes published *Mythologies*, a groundbreaking series of essays in which he analysed the popular culture of his day, from laundry detergent to the face of Greta Garbo, professional wrestling to the Citroën DS. This series of short books, Object Lessons, continues the tradition.

Melissa Harrison, *Financial Times*

PRAISE FOR *HOTEL* BY JOANNA WALSH:

A slim, sharp meditation on hotels and desire. ... Walsh invokes everyone from Freud to Forster to Mae West to the Marx Brothers. She's funny throughout, even as she documents the dissolution of her marriage and the peculiar brand of alienation on offer in lavish places.

Dan Piepenbring, *The Paris Review*

Evocative ... Walsh's strange, probing book is all the more affecting for eschewing easy resolution.

Publishers Weekly

Walsh's writing has intellectual rigour and bags of formal bravery ... *Hotel* is a boldly intellectual work that repays careful reading. Its semiotic wordplay, circling prose and experimental form may prove a refined taste, but in its deft delineation of a complex modern phenomenon—and, perhaps, a modern malaise—it's a great success.

Melissa Harrison, *Financial Times*

Walsh has been praised to the skies by Chris Kraus and Jeff Vandermeer, and it isn't hard to see why. Her writing sways between the tense and the absurd, as if it's hovering between this world and another.

Jonathan Sturgeon, *Flavorwire*

PRAISE FOR *DRONE* BY ADAM ROTHSTEIN:

Adam Rothstein's primer on drones covers (such themes as) the representation of drones in science fiction and popular culture. The technological aspects are covered in detail, and there is interesting discussion of the way in which our understanding of technology is grounded in historical narratives. As Rothstein writes, the attempt to draw a boundary between one technology and another often ignores the fact that new technologies are not quite as new as we think.

Christopher Coker, *Times Literary Supplement*

OBJECT LESSONS

A book series about the hidden lives of ordinary things.

Series Editors:

Ian Bogost and Christopher Schaberg

Advisory Board:

Sara Ahmed, Jane Bennett, Jeffrey Jerome Cohen, Johanna
Drucker, Raiford Guins, Graham Harman, renée hoogland,
Pam Houston, Eileen Joy, Douglas Kahn, Daniel Miller,
Esther Milne, Timothy Morton, Kathleen Stewart,
Nigel Thrift, Rob Walker, Michele White.

In association with

BOOKS IN THE SERIES

Remote Control by Caetlin Benson-Allott
Golf Ball by Harry Brown
Driver's License by Meredith Castile
Drone by Adam Rothstein
Silence by John Biguenet
Glass by John Garrison
Phone Booth by Ariana Kelly
Refrigerator by Jonathan Rees
Waste by Brian Thill
Hotel by Joanna Walsh
Hood by Alison Kinney
Dust by Michael Marder
Shipping Container by Craig Martin
Cigarette Lighter by Jack Pendarvis
Bookshelf by Lydia Pyne
Bread by Scott Cutler Shershow (forthcoming)
Tree by Matthew Battles (forthcoming)
Hair by Scott Lowe (forthcoming)
Password by Martin Paul Eve (forthcoming)
Eye Chart by William Germano (forthcoming)
Questionnaire by Evan Kindley (forthcoming)
Shopping Mall by Matthew Newton (forthcoming)
Blanket by Kara Thompson (forthcoming)
Doorknob by Thomas Mical (forthcoming)
Sock by Kim Adrian (forthcoming)

shipping container

CRAIG MARTIN

BLOOMSBURY ACADEMIC
LONDON • NEW YORK • OXFORD • NEW DELHI • SYDNEY

BLOOMSBURY ACADEMIC
Bloomsbury Publishing Plc
50 Bedford Square, London, WC1B 3DP, UK
1385 Broadway, New York, NY 10018, USA
29 Earlsfort Terrace, Dublin 2, Ireland

BLOOMSBURY, BLOOMSBURY ACADEMIC and the Diana logo are
trademarks of Bloomsbury Publishing Plc

First published in 2016
Reprinted in 2017, 2021, 2022

ISBN: PB: 978-1-5013-0314-2
ePDF: 978-1-5013-0315-9
eBook: 978-1-5013-0316-6

Series: Object Lessons

Typeset by Deanta Global Publishing Services, Chennai, India

To find out more about our authors and books visit www.bloomsbury.com
and sign up for our newsletters.

For Maria

CONTENTS

INTRODUCTION: BOX CLEVER

I am writing this in a shipping container. Looking out over the dramatic landscape of Loch Long, low cloud clinging to the steep hillsides. On the water two tugboats guide a tanker towards Coulport, a storage and loading base for the United Kingdom's Trident nuclear warheads, on the west coast of Scotland. A Royal Navy (RN) boat circles the tanker. This logistical exercise, off in the mid-distance, is punctuated by three highland cows drinking from the man-made water feature that sits in front of my writing desk. This is the strange, surreal, militarized landscape that surrounds Cove Park, an organization specializing in residencies for arts professionals. Cove Park is noteworthy on many levels, especially for its striking setting, but also for the architectural experiments that dot the site. Two living 'pods' designed by the architect Andrew McAvoy sit at its heart, originally constructed in 2000 for the BBC television series *Castaway* before they were repurposed at Cove Park. In addition to these is the 'cargotecture': eighteen shipping containers that were redesigned by Eric Reynolds of Urban Space Management to provide six accommodation units and three studio spaces for residents.[1] I am sitting in one of these studio spaces, plate glass windows in front of me with a view out over the loch.

There is nothing to suggest this is a shipping container. Internally it consists of plasterboard walls, wooden flooring, floor-to-ceiling glass doors, a round porthole, electricity supply, heating and bathroom. The accommodation units are similarly configured with the addition of a small kitchen – comfortable, simple, functional. Both the accommodation and studio spaces are formed from two

FIGURE 1 Container architecture at Cove Park, Scotland.

adjoined containers, their sides removed and the units welded together. Their origins are only evident from the outside. Little attempt has been made to disguise the fact that these are shipping containers: the corrugated metal side panels, the standardized corner fittings that all shipping containers have. The original doors remain, permanently opened out to provide a modicum of privacy between the accommodation spaces. Their use as accommodation and workspaces at Cove Park is understandable: they are comparatively cheap (starting at just over $13,000 for a one-bedroom unit),[2] particularly in comparison with bespoke architectural structures. Their design, including the shape, scale and size makes them ideal spaces for human usage. When inside them the ones here at Cove Park really don't feel like shipping containers at all.

The geographical aspect at Cove Park, with the containers situated overlooking the water, is an expedient illustration of the life, or I should say lives, of the shipping container. These are amphibious objects. Their ability to be moved from one place to the other in an almost seamless fashion is part of the reason for their global rise over the last fifty years. Above all the container's primary innovation is the ability to deliver goods door to door without needing to unload them every time they are moved from ship, to trains or to trucks. As we will see, this is the central innovation known as intermodalism.[3] The militarized landscape here at Cove Park also folds back into the container's relationship to the Vietnam War,[4] as well as their current widespread use in military logistics. Their capacity to embody a vast range of different functions – other than the original intended one of transporting goods – also accounts for their ubiquity across the globe. They punctuate many a motorway journey; they trundle through rail stations on the back of freight wagons; they lie in farmers' fields and scaffolding yards where they serve as makeshift storage units and workshops; they are used as dwellings; they figure in post-Punk lyrics by The Fall.[5] They are omnipresent, but so often they are taken for granted.

The shipping container can be used as a lens to look at a range of significant social and culture shifts from the mid-to-late twentieth century to the present day. Above all this apparently simple piece of design has been central to the utter dominance of globalized trade networks, including the rise of economies such as China.[6] The effects of this have been profound, and depending on your viewpoint this may not be as positive as many economists like to suggest. This is particularly the case for those maritime workers whose lives were overturned with the coming of the container, nor for the communities who had to deal with the profound changes to the cultural lives of iconic maritime cities such as London and New York City. For the geographer David Harvey the development of the shipping container and the attendant rise of containerization was 'one of the great innovations without which we would not have had globalisation, [or] the deindustrialisation of America'.[7] This object's impact has been profound to say the least, particularly its relationship to the development of the wider infrastructural system of containerization: a system that relied upon its standardization and implementation by the International Organization for Standardization (or ISO). Personally speaking this book satisfies a lifelong curiosity with these metal boxes. Growing up in the 1980s in relative close proximity to a container port on the outskirts of London, I sat in my parents' car staring out at them as they went past on the back of trucks. There were the container ships sailing along the Thames Estuary with hundreds of them stacked in neat rows. It baffled me what was behind the doors – boxes of children's toys? Possibly nothing. I never knew. We never do. There was also wonderment at their geometric logic, so pleasing to the eye. To this day I enjoy their simplicity of design. Some ten years later while studying at art school the same aesthetic predilections led me to the work of a generation of American artists also obsessed with box-like forms. Donald Judd's work in particular spoke to the aesthetic rigour of a box, its 'rightness'. It's there in his gallery pieces, and in the furniture he also designed. It was also there in Sol LeWitt's works: series upon series, all based on the grid and the cube.[8] The circle was completed when I read Allan Sekula's book *Fish Story* in 1996, his photographic exploration of the container shipping industry, its centrality to the harsh regimes of globalized maritime labour, and its relationship with minimalist sculpture.[9] The book made absolute sense. It still does.

A small number of other books in subsequent years have addressed the significance of the shipping container to economic history and logistics management, but there has been comparatively little consideration given to specific aspects of the design, architectural and material cultural significance of the container.[10] This book explores these areas and others. Shipping containers are mundane pieces of design, everyday objects that surround us. Most design is. It's anonymous in the way that Sigfried Giedion famously studied the growth of mechanization as a form of 'anonymous history'.[11] This is one of the many reasons why design is so central to our being. It inflects upon all aspects of our lives, invigorating us through the sheer pleasure of a form that pleases, or a new device that satisfies a need, but also frustrating us when something doesn't work as well as it should. As Villem Flusser noted in his book *The Shape of Things: A Philosophy of Design*, humankind's development of tools is the history of design and thus the history of humankind itself. Design and human development are folded into one another.[12] Flusser's rendering of design rightly counters the prevailing tendency in some academic areas to view design as primarily concerned with the fashionable, the style-driven, the superfluous. This is understandable when one conceives of design through the standard guise of an aesthetic makeover: a conceptualization of design that owes so much to the influence of American car design of the 1950s, and its promotion of built-in obsolescence. And although such examples are important in their own regard for understanding the development of nascent consumer capitalism in the United States, these ideas of pure surface have been superseded by a fuller, richer conceptualization of design. The position developed by Flusser is an important one as it reflects a larger sense of what design is, as both a noun and a verb. In his hands design is the bridge between art and technology, making it the engine of cultural and social production. But this also renders design as a form of deceit: and here Flusser again articulates an important sense of the power of design. For he argues that design is the means through which 'to deceive nature by means of technology, to replace what is natural with what is artificial and build a machine out of which there comes a god who is ourselves'.[13] As he says later in the same essay, 'this is a sobering explanation', but I would argue one that offers an important rejoinder to the often-stated assertion that design is mere window dressing.[14] Designed objects directly determine our engagement with the world: this book series proves exactly that. Things control our behaviour, mediating how we travel from A to B, or open a door for example. Bruno Latour famously discusses the role played by an overhead door closer and how it changes our understanding of both the door itself and – crucially – our own bodies. The physical effort required to push open a heavy old door without a closer, in comparison to an automated revolving door, highlights the embodied action of engaging with things.[15] It also emphasizes how we take things for granted once a technological system or designed object becomes commonplace, embedded within our everyday habits and rituals.

This is precisely the case with the shipping container. As the book will discuss, whilst many people may simply ignore them, our everyday lives are utterly determined by these metal boxes – just not quite in the same way as the direct engagement we may have with a door closer, a remote control or refrigerator. We don't handle them as such. Rather we might think of the shipping container as a form of 'meta-design', a designed object that is central to the role and place of smaller-scale designed objects in our lives. Shipping containers are part of a larger scale in the network of design known as 'tertiary packaging': these are objects that literally transport other commodities around the globe.[16] Without the shipping container we wouldn't be able to change TV channels with a remote control or store food in our refrigerators: above all, containers are about the distribution of things. In a way, one of the reasons containers themselves have remained somewhat taken for granted may be precisely because they are part of global distribution networks. Such networks, consisting of trucks, ships, aircraft, telecommunications or physical infrastructure, don't quite have the glamour of the opening of the latest fashion retail store on Fifth Avenue. Nor do they have the impact of febrile political debates on, and battles over, labour relations in factories and other sites of manufacture. Distribution and the related field of logistics and supply chain management do not, on the surface at least, have the same importance as production and consumption. However, for Henri Lefebvre there is a direct relationship between the three. He notes:

> The commodity asks for nothing better than to appear. And appear it does – visible/readable, in shop windows and on display racks. Self-exhibition is its forte. Once it is apparent, there is no call to decode it; it has no need of decipherment after the fashion of the 'beings' of nature and of the imagination. And yet, once it has appeared, its mystery only deepens. Who has produced it? Who will buy it? Who will profit from its sale? Who, or for what purpose, will it serve? Where will the money go?[17]

Lefebvre offers a valuable lesson on the status of the commodity. His description highlights the inherent complexity of the commodity, from the relations of production, through its functional qualities, to the 'spectacle' of its presentation, and post-consumption rituals of ownership. Yet, there is a gap. We need to ask: How did it get to these shop windows or display racks? It didn't simply materialize. Rather, the movement of the commodity, its distribution from the point of production to the retail environment, is treated with seemingly less importance. Although later in the book Lefebvre goes on to discuss the role of commodity distribution and the importance of warehouses, trucks, trains, ships and the routes travelled, it is still quite telling that the issue of distribution per se was not raised in his initial questions.[18] It seems taken as a given: the mysteries of its ability to appear are underplayed. This was not the case in the time of the great maritime cities of the past, where the fraught lives of individuals, the cacophony of the port, and the multitude of commodities being shipped to and fro, made the transportation of goods often a thing of excitement, even occasional wonderment. The blank face of a shipping container or a distribution warehouse doesn't hold quite the same romance. But again, this is precisely why they are such important objects of study.

As we will see in this book, one of the reasons distribution has become a neglected field of enquiry is precisely due to the rise of containerization and the loss of traditional urban maritime cultures – because without distribution the raw materials for production would not be available; without distribution, consumer goods would not populate shops all over the globe. Focusing on the space of distribution is incredibly valuable as it signals the diverse range of moments and sites where distribution and circulation are so central to capitalism. As Lefebvre highlights, at one end of the scale circulation is framed around material distribution in the form of the packaging of goods, their physical distribution to warehouses, stores, shops and markets. At the other end, there is the circulation of information through marketing, advertising, mail-order catalogues, trade fairs and online environments. Of course the latter areas have been widely studied, particularly advertising and marketing, but the physical distribution of things to a much lesser extent. We could take a range of examples: from the distribution of parcels through global courier companies, to the architecture of warehouses and distribution centres. But it is the shipping container that links together so many aspects of distributive space. Above all then my interest in distributive space – and the container as one of the key facets of this – lies in the ultimate power it has to mediate our daily lives in relation to contemporary capitalism.

Shipping containers and angels. On the surface there isn't much in common between them: one a steel box, the other a divine messenger in the monotheistic and polytheistic traditions. But these are both mobile, both medial things. For the French philosopher Michel Serres angels are a potent metaphor for global communication. They are messengers who carry messages flittingly through the ether, often revealing themselves unannounced. In his book *Angels: A Modern Myth*, Serres constructs an intricate meshwork of connections between these religious messengers – satellite communication technology; speech acts; the movement of objects and transportation technologies such as supersonic aircraft. From this perspective he suggests that 'when people, aircraft and electronic signals are transmitted through the air, they are all effectively messages and messengers'.[19] This is an image of globalization, of a multiplicity of information flying around in our midst, without us necessarily aware of its presence. The approach I take to the shipping container is partly in keeping with Serres' curiosity about angels. For me the container is a potent paradigm of the age we live in: of the informational might of big data, coupled with the fact that the stuff we consume travels around in these 4-ton boxes. Serres' image of a world of medial transmission is there in big data and big boxes, both carriers of information and goods.[20]

For Serres, objects are always spatial, constituting the space around us. His use of the term 'spatial character' is important as it also emphasizes the interpersonal drama that unfolds every time we engage with objects. To highlight the choreography between people and objects he offers the example of a rugby match, or we might think of a game of football: rather than the players being the point of focus as may typically be the case, Serres suggests that we need to follow the ball. For the ball is 'a tracker of relations'.[21] The object traces the complexity of the game's spatial relations: it can be read through the interaction between the ball and the players. Likewise we might conceive of the shipping container in a similar manner, by tracking the relations of the container and its object-geographies as way of understanding the complexities of distributive space. There are many ways to look at the shipping container, to learn lessons from it. I want to think of the container as a 'spatial character' in the way that Serres does – one that pops up in an array of narratives[22]: from the growth of automation in the late nineteenth and early twentieth centuries; the rise of standardization; the power and dominance of infrastructural design; the critical importance of everyday design technologies; the de-industrialization of western economies and the development of the global south and Far East; to the geopolitical insecurities of the present day.

1 A TIGHT STOW

'Ropes. Ropes. Ropes. Stay stronger – Longer!'[1]

An advert by the London Spinning Company shows a black and white stylized scene with loose planks of timber being manoeuvred onboard a ship. A man stands on the dockside, the timber winched above him, attached by ropes. Ropes are everywhere (perhaps unsurprisingly given the remit of the advert). On board the vessel another man stands in silhouette, guiding the load of timber. Looking at the image alone it is difficult to ascertain the date of the scene: it could be any time from the nineteenth century onwards.

Another advertisement – 'Stothert & Pitt. Container Handling Cranes' – another black and white stylized depiction. This time the images are stark in their exactness. Three schematic drawings of large-scale cranes, neat boxes stacked below them. These are images of efficiency. The copy continues:

Immense capital investments depend on the efficiency and reliability of container handling cranes. The unique experience of STOTHERT & PITT in crane engineering results in designs which are matched to operating requirements and provides the right appliance for each project. Stothert & Pitt quay and marshalling yard cranes for containers add a new chapter to their proud record as crane-makers to the world's Ports.[2]

Even the language speaks of order: efficiency; reliability; operating requirements; the *right* appliance. All carried out under the economic eye of capital investment. It is much easier to date this advertisement. Both the schematic drawings and the design of the advert itself, including the sans serif typeface, locate it squarely in the 1960s.

These advertisements, both from the May 1967 issue of *The PLA Monthly*, the Port of London Authority magazine, describe an industry in transition. They conjure a shift in focus. One a link to the rich genealogy of port cities around the globe: hives of activity with loose break-bulk cargo being manoeuvred, noise, smell, life; the other an ordered world of efficiency to come: automated movement, devoid of the texture of maritime cultures of old. The date of 1967 is interesting. At this point the freight shipping industry in both the UK and other western economies was undergoing significant change due to the impact of technological advancement, particularly the growing importance of containerized freight.

Even seven years later the December 1974 edition of *The PLA Monthly* still featured advertisements and articles that showed a mix of traditional freight handling methods alongside containerized practices. One article, eulogizing the role of the Port of London Authority in boosting the United Kingdom's export activities, describes 'the expertise of the PLA dockers who initially unload the exports from lorry, handle them safely, from small compact cartons to large unwieldy pieces of machinery'.[3] Tellingly the dockworkers deal with a wide array of export goods, in differing shapes and sizes. The article also shows images of Jaguar motorcars being winched on board; wooden boxes attached to cranes; metal cylinders of chemical products waiting on the dockside; sailing yachts propped up on wooden pallets, ready to be winched on board. All separate pieces of cargo. In addition, the magazine features an advertisement for the Port of London Authority's new container handling facility at Tilbury on the outskirts of London (the port close to where I grew up). Opened in 1967, the advert extols the efficiency of operations at the Port of Tilbury. It is about speed above all else. The port operates twenty-four hours a day, all year round; it conducts a two-shift, fourteen-hour working day; and it offers 'the highest degree of mechanisation for the speedy handling of palletised, unitised and containerised cargo'.[4] In contrast with the loose items of metal cylinders and motor vehicles in the article from the same issue, the photographs in this advertisement show only the blank faces of shipping containers. We have no idea what they contain.

By 1984 this had changed again. Looking at an issue of the same magazine, now renamed *Port of London*, the second edition from 1984 no longer features the mix of traditional freight handling processes, and containerized techniques. Containers dominate. They abound. The editorial for the magazine offers a celebratory tone due to the seventy-fifth anniversary of the establishment of the Port of London Authority itself, but there is also a creeping atmosphere of despondency. The United Kingdom's reputation as the 'warehouse of the world' had disappeared. The business of shipping had changed due to new industrial relations, and fundamentally, the impact of the new cargo handling technologies associated with containerization had led to the loss of the PLA's supremacy. Whilst this focus on the activities of the Port of London Authority provides just one example from the United Kingdom, the illustration of the gradual shift from traditional mechanized techniques of handling freight to the dominance of containerization is a useful starting point to consider the 'container revolution'.[5]

The handling of freight has long been an arduous form of labour, as well as highly skilled of course. One of the most compelling evocations of this, and the momentous changes to come, is the 1963 book *Men and Machines: A Story About Longshoring on the West Coast Waterfront*.[6] Not only is this is a handsome object in its own right it's a vivid account of the tense battles over the future of the shipping industry and the devastating impact of mechanization on the longshoring labour force. Interestingly the book is a joint publication between the Pacific Maritime Association (representing ship owners) and the International Longshoremen's and

Warehousemen's Union (representing workers in the industry), outlining the agreement on mechanization and modernization in the ports of California, Oregon and Washington. It's also a memento of a time now long gone, depicting the gradual shift from traditional methods of handling freight to the exponential growth of mechanized techniques. As with the advertisements above, 1963 is a time of transition in the shipping industry, where certain age-old methods of handling are still in place.[7] A case in point is the continued use of the longshoreman's hook: a simple tool that effectively extends the longshoreman's hand, allowing him to manoeuvre 500-pound bales of jute with comparative ease. Whilst such implements may seem almost archaic in design, the point is that as extensions of man (in the sense of Marshall McLuhan's work) these are already forms of mechanization. And mechanization is about increasing speed and efficiency. But it is primarily concerned with the move away from 'complicated handicraft' to the domination of the machine.[8] The rest of *Men and Machines* depicts the increasing use of mechanized equipment to take some of the burden off the workers, including rope slings, and four-wheeler wagons to transport cargo in ship's holds. These wagons were not new. They had been in use for over fifty years, suggesting that the ultimate impact of mechanization was gestating for quite some time.[9] Indeed there are numerous cases of early forms of mechanized freight handling. As early as 1888, for example, photographs show the use of dockside hydraulic cranes to winch goods from ship to shore,[10] whilst another advertisement in the Port of London Authority magazine from April 1929 shows the use of a pneumatic plant for loading and discharging grain onto and off of ships. Again, this is all about increasing the speed of loading, with the advert extolling the number of tons per hour that the machine could handle.

For all the moves towards full-scale mechanization of cargo handling, the key problem for the shipping industry in this period was still the individualized nature of cargo itself. Although a mechanical crane, for example, could alleviate some of the back-breaking lifting for the longshoremen, without the consolidation of the cargo itself the loading procedures were never going to be as efficient as they might be. If we consider again the pneumatic grain plant advert from 1929, the crucial factor here is that the nature of grain is such that it can flow almost like a liquid, whereas the problem with individual logs or animal carcasses for instance is that they are always singular, loose items; they can't flow in the same way as grain or oil. And whilst materials such as paper replaced burlap and jute sacking in order to improve the working conditions of longshoremen, the fact remained that sacks themselves had to be handled individually. The primary factor with individual items of cargo was the time required to load these in the hold of a ship. One image from *Men and Machines* depicts the diversity of goods on board one vessel: hundreds of cardboard boxes of numerous shapes and sizes; bales of jute neatly tucked in next to the cardboard boxes; next to these again some 'U'-shaped objects, whose purpose is difficult to ascertain. The art of the longshoreman was in understanding the relationship between the shape and size of individual items of cargo, and the most efficient place in the ships' hold for them to be placed. It was a long-crafted, skill-based knowledge of how the hold could be loaded in order to provide a 'tight stow'.[11] The complexity of loading and stowing is most clearly demonstrated by looking at cargo planning diagrams from this period in the mid-twentieth century. One in particular from 1960 demonstrates the sheer multiplicity of cargo in the hold of the *Kipling*, which sailed from various ports in South America to the United Kingdom:

Casks of tallow; 45 tons of fruit; 57 tons of tinned meat; 500 dry hides; wool; horsehair (wings); tins of fruit; 1479 cases of meat; 247 bales of cotton; 763 pieces of timber; 249 tons of wheat; 76 tons of lard; 60 tons of canned meat; 100 tons of coffee; 305 tons chilled beef; 1243 carcases of lamb; 413 bags of offal; 657 cases of offal; 2112 carcases of lamb; 356 tons of frozen beef; 178 tons of linseed expellers; 987 tons of wet hides; 138 tones of timber; bags of coffee; 95 tons tinned meats; 276 tons of chilled beef; 1433 bags of wheat; 812 tons of bulk wheat; 83 tons of meal; tins of fruit; casks of tallow; 106 tons of cotton; 103 tons of linters; 4237 pieces of timber; 3006 cases of meat; 646 casks of lard; bales of cotton; 60 tons of quebracho extract; 164 tons of dried blood; and, finally, 1370 bags of bones.[12]

This is one vessel setting sail on 1 September 1960, making ports of call at Cardiff, Liverpool and Glasgow. Not only does this lengthy list outline the utter diversity of goods being shipped from South America to the United Kingdom, it demonstrates the complexity of loading and unloading all these disparate items. The correct distribution of weight was a critical factor in enabling vessels to sail safely without listing. Equally, the distribution of cargo in the hold allowed for the most efficient offloading at a ship's various ports of call. Added to this the loading patterns of the hold meant that the ideal number of longshoremen could be employed to unload the cargo.[13] Whilst the remit of the cargo plans and the stow of the hold itself were to provide the quickest turnaround times for vessels loading and unloading at ports, this was often a lengthy process. For example, in 1963 for a vessel carrying 6,500 tons the total man-hours required to discharge and load with traditional cargo loading and handling techniques was just over 11,000, with an actual turnaround time of the vessel in port, five and a half days. Compare this with early forms of shipping containers. For the equivalent tonnage it required 850 total man-hours to load and unload, and forty hours in port.[14] The economics of this are plain to see, at least for the ship's owners and the port operators. *Men and Machines* is an account of the dwindling need for the longshoremen labour force. Whilst mechanization was a decisive factor in the significant social, economic, political and cultural changes to the shipping industry in this period, it was the move away from loose, individual items of cargo towards unitized and regularized cargo that was equally as significant. And this is where the story of the standardized shipping container has its tentative beginnings.

The wooden pallet: as with the majority of useful objects, they are simple and easily ignored. They are made up of sections of cheap, often recycled, wood nailed together in a straightforward fashion. In the history of the shipping container the pallet plays an important interim role, prefiguring in many ways the economic and spatial logic that ultimately led to the standardized box we know today.[15] The principle of unitization is to simplify and regularize the shape of individual items of break-bulk cargo to make them more manageable, and easier to transport. For one container historian 'the ideal is an unbroken door-to-door service'.[16] Whilst the use of sacking made the movement of loose items a little easier, it was the introduction of pallets in the 1930s that made the manoeuvrability of cargo easier still, but particularly their use by the US Army in the early 1940s that signalled their potential to reduce handling and loading times.[17] Rather than sacks of goods being handled individually, pallets allowed multiple sacks to be stacked on top of one another and winched onto or off of ships. Whilst this may seem obvious to us today, the introduction of the pallet was decisive in changing the procedures for handling cargo. By homogenizing and, crucially, scaling up the shape of break-bulk cargo it meant that more cargo could be moved at a quicker pace. Another advertisement from the May 1967 issue of *The PLA Monthly* mentioned above features the benefits of pallets: 'Save man-hours. Cut costs. Equally at home on truck or crane, takes goods right from shed to ship without reloading.'[18] The latter point was significant. No longer did dockworkers need to move goods from the warehouse or shed to the dockside, then transfer the goods onto the ship, then reload and stow them in the ship's hold. Palletized goods could be moved by forklift from the shed, winched onto the ship then moved into place in ships' holds by another forklift. Quicker, simpler, fewer people required. You can see where this is going.

In the same year as the pallets advert, the UK government under the British Board of Trade commissioned a report by the management consultants McKinsey & Co. into the potential economic advantages of full-scale containerization. This was titled *Containerization: The Key to Low-Cost Transport.*[19] The report notes how the use of pallets represents an intermediate stage in the move towards a full-scale system of containerization.[20] The regularization of break-bulk cargoes was seen to provide quicker turnaround times, greater labour productivity, and reduced costs. However, the report also identified a number of drawbacks with pallets. Although they sped up the process of handling cargo, this only went so far due to the limitations on the size of the pallets themselves and the volume of cargo they could carry. For instance they were much more suited to small-scale sacks and other similar sized domestic products, as opposed to large-scale industrial machinery. The key factor was size: increase their scale further still and you could cut loading times and labour costs. Although it was positive about the use of pallets, the McKinsey report basically makes the case for the use of sealed containers. Where the typical reduction in labour costs was 7 tons per man-hour for pallets in comparison with non-palletized cargo, for fully enclosed containers this rose to savings of over 50 tons per man-hour.[21] Further still, enclosed containers also offered better protection from damage to the cargo, often from longshoremen's hooks, and potential theft by dockworkers.

Containers have been used as transportation units for centuries, the most obvious example being the barrel.[22] They offer a way of consolidating a wide range of different materials, be they liquids such as alcohol, or foodstuffs like olives. Once contained in the barrel the disparate material qualities become homogenized, made identical. On the outside all barrels are ostensibly the same. Containment is a form of ordering. As a standard homogenized unit the barrel provided greater ease of measurement, storage and transportation.[23] Nevertheless on the latter point the shape of barrels was not entirely conducive to transportation in ships' holds: whilst they can be stowed on their sides and laid one on top of the other in a staggered, tile-like fashion, the bottom layer needs to be shored up through the use of dunnage to fill in the gaps where the top of the barrel lies. Likewise at the end of the row, the gap left by the staggering required further use of dunnage to fill the gaps and provide added stability.[24] The key drawback with barrels is their shape. This is where the cubic geometry of the box comes into its own. A simple box: these forgettable pieces of commonplace design that we rely upon so much, to store things away under the bed; to carry groceries to the car; or to consolidate items in our kitchen cupboards. As 'daily technologies of containment' boxes allow us to organize space and the movement of things.[25] This is precisely the organizational logic behind the use of box-shaped containers in common domestic settings, but equally in the distribution of goods across the globe. Even though the standardized, ISO intermodal shipping container is now so emblematic of global transportation networks, the use of boxes as transportation containers has been in existence for quite some time. The exact dates of the first emergence of containers that facilitated the transloading of goods are widely debated. Some state that this was at least since the 1830s when they were used on the rail network in the United Kingdom between the cities of Liverpool and Manchester.[26] This continued in the mid-late nineteenth century when railway companies in Britain and France used wooden boxes on flatbed wagons.[27] Similarly, in the first years of the twentieth century the use of 'lift-vans' was also seen, where they offered 'immediate loading in any city in the United States or in Europe' and ensure 'a minimum of handling, security for small packages, and least possible risk of damage'.[28] This sounds very familiar. Although some argue that little progress was made in the shipping industry in the 1920s, other scholars point out that the railroads were forging ahead in the use of transhipment containers or 'vans' during this period. From 1921 a rail service of containerized freight began to operate between Cleveland and Chicago, before extending services to New York, New Jersey, Pennsylvania, Massachusetts and Ohio.[29] The key point with these examples of containerized rail transport is that they offered early forms of intermodal, door-to-door delivery. As with ISO shipping containers today, they could be packed at the producer's warehouse, delivered to the rail depot, loaded on board, transported to the intermediate destination, offloaded and unpacked at the final destination – all without the contents being touched.[30]

These early transhipment containers were effectively scaled-up metal versions of simple wooden or cardboard boxes. A survey of photographs from the 1950s as well as the 1960s is revealing. One example of containerized cargo shipments includes the Link-Line service between Liverpool-Belfast, United Kingdom, started in January 1959. This service used 12-ton capacity aluminium containers, but these were non-standard in design and used rounded top edges.[31] A further example, developed by Shield Transport Systems, is approximately 8 feet cubed, formed of smooth metal and fixed with rivets, a single door, but without any hooks or anchor points on the top, and is manoeuvred by a standard forklift.[32] Another from 1966, operated by African Container Express, looks ostensibly the same size and proportion, although this time has anchor points on the top four corners, allowing a lifting frame to be attached to a crane.[33] The momentous changes happening to the shipment of freight at this time are there to see in this example: the container has a Mobil banner attached to it stating 'First shipment of oil to Nigeria by through-container'. It is also evident that the nomenclature for 'shipping containers' had also still to be agreed upon. The term 'through-container' is useful as an illustration of how the container could be loaded up at the point of origin and travel all the way through to its destination without being unloaded, as would previously have been the case. Like Mobil, the Ford Motor Company utilized metal containers to deliver spare parts: in this case the smooth metal container in question was again approximately 8 feet cubed, with chamfered top corners and hooked eyelets for attaching to a crane.[34] One further example of the differing container designs in use during the 1960s is the Gilbey container. This particular design is smaller than the ones used by African Container Express, approximately 5 feet cubed, with corrugated metal used on all surfaces and rounded corners. Hooked eyelets can again be seen in use for hoisting by crane.[35]

These were hardy objects, protecting the goods within both from damage during shipment and from the longshoremen's hooks. In March 1967 an 'experiment' was staged which illustrates just this, consisting of the first-ever shipment of Japanese canned red salmon from Japan to London in one of the early designs of the shipping container. On the *Chitral*'s arrival into London's King George V Dock on 25 April, the director of the importers stated: 'I have never seen cans which have travelled 10,000 miles in such excellent condition.'[36] We take such things for granted today of course, but it is telling how significant an event this was even as recently as the late 1960s. When the container was discharged from the ship it took eight men to guide the container onto the back of a waiting truck. This is also notable, for on the one hand it highlights how human labour was still necessary to offload the container, whilst more decisively illustrating how the partial *interchangeability* of the container was at work. As with the Africa Container Express through-container, the enclosed design of the container allowed it to be loaded straight onto the truck without its contents being held in storage or packed separately. It was noted that the container 'was in Manchester housewives' larder within 24 hours. … One load went directly to Wright & Green Ltd., Manchester, from where it will be distributed to the Spar chain of grocers.'[37]

It's clear then that the shipment of goods in containers was not new. However, whilst these various examples of container designs were ostensibly the same (similar size, materials, openings, attachments), *they weren't similar enough*. Although the containers homogenized and regularized the contents, the containers themselves were not regularized. There was too much diversity. Various shipping companies used different containers, and this meant that each container had to be handled and moved differently. Some containers could be lifted using specially designed bars; others had to be hoisted using ropes lashed around them. Ultimately this slowed the process due to a lack of interchangeability or modularity. With this 'accelerationist' mentality comes the desire for ultimate speed – things had to be quicker and quicker. There was also the question of economies of scale: Why use an 8-foot-cubed box when you could use an even larger one that stored more cargo and could be moved fewer times? This is the exact argument made in the 1967 McKinsey & Co. report: the key factor that would offer integration and economies of scale was the *standardization* of the container so that a globally recognized design could be developed.[38] Five years prior to this, in 1962, one commentator neatly summarized the problem:

> Most types of liquids and solids may someday be moved in sealed containers interchangeable among road, rail, air, and marine transport. Advantages would include reduction in damage and loss in the time and cost of loading and unloading. Containers may prove to be the catalyst that integrates the various components of the transport sector which are now being independently planned, financed, and operated.[39]

How correct he was, both in terms of the fact that most goods are now moved in sealed containers (90 per cent of the worlds' goods), and that containers proved to be the object that changed the freight transport industry – and so much more.

2 TEU

There is an image from the first decade of the twentieth century that shows the inventor of the telephone, Alexander Graham Bell, standing next to a large tetrahedral kite structure built out of octet truss forms. Bell was interested in the potential of kites as aerial vehicles.[1] I've always found this image temporally troubling but absolutely fascinating. He stands wearing clothing typical of the period: a worker's jacket, tie, Breton cap.[2] It's the presence of this alien structure next to him that intrigues me. Whilst he is very much of the time – particularly his moustache – the structure looks to be from a future age, arrived out of nowhere. There is also something illusory about the object: it plays with the surface of the image, destabilizing our reading of the picture plane itself. The two look to be from different centuries, time conflated, folded in this one moment.

A similar historical coupling takes place when I see images of shipping containers from the 1960s being manoeuvred using old techniques and technologies. The design of the shipping container that is essentially the same as today's has its roots in the mid-1950s, but the infrastructure to handle

FIGURE 2 Alexander Graham Bell's multi-celled kite frame, early 1900s.

these early containers had not been developed alongside the design of the container itself. Images from the mid-late 1960s depict the now-familiar metal containers being tied onto the backs of flatbed trucks in much the same way as any other type of load would have been. The containers appear to be out of time, released onto an unsuspecting world too soon. In this image a traditional hoist lowers the container, ropes reaching around it. A group of dockworkers guide it down by hand, as it nestles onto the back of a truck not specifically designed for containers. Others (possibly

FIGURE 3 Container handling at Victoria Docks, Port of London, 1966.

managers) stand slightly back, almost quizzical about the scene. This is understandable given that the container was part of an experimental shipment of canned fruit from Australia to London in 1966. It is all very much improvised with little evidence of a *system* being in place. For it is the importance placed on a standardized system that is so crucial to the history and power of the shipping container. This is containerization.

The standardized shipping container is a simple object. A box, or rather a '*revolutionized* box'.[3] As we saw in

Chapter 1, the idea of a box or container of stuff being transported is an age-old practice, 'a concept as timeless as transportation itself'.[4] What then is so *revolutionary* about this particular box? Put simply, it is the fact that its size, shape and form were agreed upon, made standard, and applied on a near-universal basis. But more than this it was also the fact that the entire infrastructure that enabled these boxes to be transported so efficiently was also changed and standardized to a great extent. The process of standardization and universal agreement by the shipping industry as a whole finally meant that goods could be delivered door to door – from the factory or warehouse to the retail outlet without being slowed down by unnecessary delays when being transferred across different types of transport. This is the concept of *intermodal* transport that now defines the standardized shipping container.

Although the economic history of the shipping container has been written before, in order to appreciate the significance of the structural changes that led to the development of the standardized intermodal container we have to return to 1953. As we saw in the last chapter, whilst the nascent forms of the sealed container offered numerous advantages, one of the key drawbacks was the lack of an integrated system to move and handle the containers in an efficient manner. The old ropes to lash these boxes onto trucks or rail cars slowed the process down, as did the diversity of container designs. For transportation scholars reflecting on this early period, one of the most significant problems that required resolving was the need for a *standardized system* that could be recognized globally across the wide range of operators who were part of the shipping industry.[5] These included the manufacturers themselves, the road hauliers responsible for goods delivery, freight forwarding companies, shipping agents, rail network operators, and stevedoring or longshoring companies, all of whom effectively operated in isolation.[6] So, without the technical changes possible through standardizing the system itself, as well as the structural changes to the disaggregated industry, the economic imperative of moving towards sealed containers was limited. As McKinsey & Co. saw it:

> The need to look upon transport as an integrated process from origin to destination and the potential economies of scale achievable with high volumes will eventually lead to the emergence of a small number of large organizations operating on a worldwide basis.[7]

However, achieving a fully standardized container and attendant system was fraught. Marc Levinson's rigorous outline of the development of the standardized container offers a detailed account of the move towards standardization, superseding other testimonies which tend to take the notion of standardization as a given – this is central to the global dominance of the container. It's widely recognized that the person who was responsible for the nascent development of the shipping container was the US truck operator Malcom McLean.[8] At this time in 1953 McLean's aim was to overcome the problem of congested highways on the US east coast. To do so he proposed the idea of transporting truck trailers on ships rather than trucks. Today this doesn't seem terribly revolutionary, but bear in mind again the fact that the freight transport industry was far from consolidated. Crucially, in this period the truck and ship industries were completely separate so there was little obligation for the two sectors to cooperate and work together in overcoming congestion, as they were in competition.[9] There were, however, limitations to such a proposal, most notably, the problem of trying to transport truck trailers on board ships with their chassis and wheels still attached. As with the stowage of barrels or other similar items, the irregular shape of the truck trailers meant that space was unused beneath the trailer chassis. This was just wasted space, and thus costly. However, if the trailer wheels were removed, this spatial wastage could be eliminated. Perhaps more fundamentally it also meant that the trailers would be able to be stacked one on top of the other.[10] Such a development was important, for it overcame the problem of wasted space. But whilst this was crucial, such a solution did not differ markedly from the system of using unitized sealed boxes. McLean's major recognition was that the system as a *whole* needed to be reconfigured and reorganized to enable the demounted trailer bodies to be moved across different forms of transport, that is, trucks, ships, rail. His decision to separate the truck trailer and box may not seem of revolutionary significance, but this meant that the previous divergence of road, rail and sea networks might finally be overcome.[11]

In March 1955 McLean commissioned the container engineer Keith Tantlinger to design a new container. The proposed container was to be 33 feet in length, noticeably longer than previous designs that, as we saw in Chapter 1, tended to be around 8 feet long. Added to this, a decommissioned T-2 type tanker, the *Ideal-X*, was reconfigured to accommodate the new containers. Given the earlier examples of unitized container cargo, one of the decisive factors in McLean's operation was his realization that not only would the container itself have to be designed from the outset, but more importantly so would the entire infrastructure, including the ships themselves and the system of container handling.[12] This is the critical point. On the decommissioned tanker, for example, the idea was to refit the deck with a metal armature that would allow the containers to be lowered into the framework without a longshoreman required to stow them.[13] The cells, as they are known, did away with previous design of stowage decks on break-bulk ships where smaller interconnected spaces were used. In container ships the cells effectively run throughout the entire length of the ship above and below deck. The fears of the longshoremen in *Men and Machines* were well founded. In terms of cargo handling equipment, where previously various non-standardized containers would be lifted via shipboard winches, McLean opted to refit two existing dockside cranes, moving them to the ports where the first container-ship journey would be made. The key reason for using dockside cranes rather than the shipboard ones was the increased weight of the larger containers that could potentially undermine the stability of the vessel.[14]

The date of 26 April 1956 is significant – it was the first sailing of the *Ideal-X* from Newark to Houston.[15] The reason this is important is because the journey prefigured the momentous shifts that would occur not only throughout the shipping industry, but also across the entire freight transport industry as a whole: trucks, trains and ships, as well as the structural changes to the urban geographies of traditional maritime cities. Ultimately, the importance of McLean's approach to the development of the intermodal shipping container lay with his realization that the complete system of transportation had to be reconfigured. This relied upon the standardization and regularization of procedures and materials across the whole industry, thus ensuring the compatibility of the various sectors of road, rail and maritime transportation. The 1967 McKinsey & Co. report argued that this was precisely the structural, paradigm shift that was needed – including commentary on how these changes would also result in reduced insurance premiums for shipping companies. They also suggested that without a standardized design 'nonstandard containers by themselves are just another form of unitisation similar to pallets'.[16]

Although the early experiments of McLean and his company were recognized for their potential economic benefit, any cross-industry-wide agreement was a long time coming.[17] This was primarily down to cold, hard competition. Although the concept of containerization had, by the mid-1960s, become widely accepted as the future of freight transport, various companies had adopted an array of different sizes, some 20 feet in length, others 30, 35 or 40.[18] The now widely recognized standard sizes of the 'twenty-foot equivalent' (or TEU) shipping container (8 feet wide, 8 feet 6 inches high) were only fully agreed upon as late as 1970 by the ISO.[19] The phrase 'twenty-foot equivalent' is telling, for although the 20-foot version is the baseline, the ISO shipping container is available in a range of sizes including 10, 30, 40 and 45 feet. There are also high-cube versions with a height of 9 feet 6 inches. Although there are variations in size, the important aspect about standardization is that they are compatible. This is also the case with the different functions of containers: tanktainers for example are cylindrical tanks for carrying bulk cargo such as liquids, but these are framed by an armature of the standard container sizes and corner fittings.

Whilst these may now be accepted industry standards, it is worth recalling the two adverts from 1967 discussed in the previous chapter: one an image of tradition with loose cargo being winched onto a vessel, the other a picture of order and efficiency. This was an industry on the cusp of change. But the extent and speed of this change was still being fought over. Although the initial sizes were agreed upon in 1961, it was only after 1966 that the various interested parties in the shipping industry began to compromise and cooperate with one another.[20] To a certain extent this is understandable given the diverse approaches of the various agencies involved. For example, in the United States in the late 1960s the inward and outward transportation of cargo was overseen by three different agencies, depending on which mode of transport was employed. Added to this, in 1967 the Department of Transportation was set up in order to institute a national transportation strategy. For historians of this period it was clear that any major technical developments had to go hand in hand with structural integration.[21] The primary reason the sizes of the containers themselves had to be agreed upon was the need for compatibility: if the container sizes varied significantly then it was nigh on impossible to develop a *global* freight transportation network. As noted in 1967: 'The world system of containerisation ... cannot work economically or technically with a multitude of container sizes.'[22] Central to this is the standardization of infrastructure.

We will consider the broader impact of the global infrastructure of containerization in the next chapter, but it's worth dwelling just briefly on its wider role here. Infrastructure has been central to the mobilization of political, military, as well as commercial power for centuries, so much so that the Roman army recognized the importance of well-maintained roads to provide them with effective lines of communication and supply.[23] More recently the architectural scholar Keller Easterling has elaborated on the centrality of infrastructure space to the pursuit of contemporary neoliberal agendas, going as far as describing infrastructures such as global broadband networks as forms of 'extrastatecraft', meaning that the owners and operators of such infrastructures hold as much power as nation-states, but on an extra-state basis.[24] Containerization might be thought of in a similar vein. Again, this is something we will turn to in the next chapter. For now the focus remains on the technical developments that led to the growth of container handling infrastructures. Vital to the structural integration was the standardized nature of infrastructure, enabling the coupling of the container to a variety of different forms of transport – ship, road and rail. These developments included significant technical advances, such as the previously mentioned design of container-cell ships built to accommodate containers in specially designed cell bays on the vessels. There was also the redesign of road haulage vehicles to enable them to handle containers. This effectively did away with the familiar flatbed of a truck trailer, replaced with a framework including retractable twist-lock mechanisms. Further infrastructural design included railway rolling stock; the design of container handling vehicles in ports; the design and construction of large-scale dockside gantry cranes and the design of spreader bars – essentially a metal frame for lifting containers. Marc Levinson notes that Tantlinger's design for the bars enabled the container to be lifted without the need for dockworkers to attach rope to the container or crane. This device meant that 'once the box had been lifted and moved, another flip of the switch would disengage the hooks, without a worker on the ground touching the container'.[25] The later patented Universal Lifting Spreader from 1969 is an invention intended to overcome certain limitations in the compatibility between lifting gear and the various sizes of container. The patent states:

In order to provide a truly universal lifting spreader for handling all sizes and all types of cargo containers, it is necessary to provide a lifting spreader which can engage any one of the five standard sizes of cargo containers by means of top lift twist locks or bottom lift grapples.[26]

Whilst this may not be the most poetic piece of prose, it is a valuable snapshot of the development of the infrastructure in the late 1960s. Up to this point the design of lifting spreaders had been such that they could only lift specific sizes of container, limiting the scope of the types of containers that could be lifted at any one time. The word universal is decisive, for it meant that the lifting procedures could be carried out and repeated in container ports the world over. Given the move towards the automation of container handling with devices such as the spreader bar, we see how the elimination of human labour in this part of the process echoes the wider elimination of human labour through mechanization and automation. Crucially the effort expended by the longshoreman – and of course the skill – is redirected or *delegated* to technology: this would have a huge impact on labour relations in the shipping industry, and beyond.

With the internecine debates on the move to containeri-zation, the ultimate result was that everything had to be effectively designed from scratch. Interestingly for the discussion in the Introduction regarding the importance of distributive space to consumer capitalism, at this period in the late 1960s design literature frequently focused on technical innovations in the transportation sectors. For example, *Design*, the in-house journal of the United Kingdom's Council of Industrial Design, ran numerous articles on new designs for cargo handling vehicles, cranes and other distribution technologies. One significant part of the standardized ISO intermodal container that exemplifies the importance of design is the container corner fitting and the related twist-lock mechanism. As noted above, the key point is that the container had to be able to be attached to a range of different vehicles and fit into a range of spaces. The design of the corner fitting enables this. Like much of what befits containerization, to look at this corner fitting doesn't immediately fill one with the aesthetic wonder of looking at piece of high-Modernist architecture, or the pleasing symbolic functionality of a Dieter Rams domestic product. But the corner fitting *is* significant because it allows the container to be used across various forms of transport. The design of the corner fitting was approved in September 1965,[27] and covered by ISO 1161. They consist of four on top and four on the bottom of the container, with an elongated oblong hole on the upper and lower faces, and two shorter oblong holes on each outer-facing corner; they are made of steel, stainless steel or aluminium, and their placement on the corners of the container is covered by a standard spacing of 2,260 millimetres in width, so that various means of lifting containers can also be standardized across road, rail and sea. Effectively, we might think of the corner fitting as a 'bridging device' that allows the container to be attached to lifting apparatuses, such as spreader bars or port gantry cranes. Just as importantly they facilitate a secure fastening to truck trailers, and on board container-cell ships where they are locked onto the ship's loading bay armatures. The issue of affixing is crucial, for the twist-lock mechanism is required to secure the container via the corner fitting through a simple, but critical, locking device. The holes in the corner fittings engage the stub of the twist locks, which can then simply be turned, locking the container in place. This is design at its best – a straightforward device that facilitates such a seemingly inconsequential act of locking the container in place, but at the same time an act with such profound implications. In contrast to the corner fitting, the twist locks themselves are non-standard designs, and the UK Health and Safety Executive notes that as of 2008 some forty-six designs of manual and semi-automatic twist locks were in use.[28] This, they suggest, has resulted in a diversity of designs (including left-handed and right-handed mechanisms) but also a lack of safety. Amongst the variety of twist-lock designs available there is a mix of manual, semi-automatic (where the lock engages automatically when the container is lowered into position, but has to be manually disengaged) and fully automatic twist locks (where the process of disengagement is achieved by a slight twist of the container as it is moved by a gantry crane). The apparently mundane design of the corner fitting (and the twist lock) demonstrates how important connection and linkage (both materially and conceptually) are to the intermodal nature of containerization, the ideal of the 'unbroken door-to-door service'.[29]

Modularity and standardization

One other way of thinking about the importance of the way that containers can be repeatedly moved across different modes of transport is through the notion of modularity. Modular design is a system where individual parts can be linked together so that over a period of time parts can be added (or removed) as desired. An obvious example is a furniture system. Take the scenario where a consumer purchases a storage unit: they initially need only a small number of units for their limited possessions, but over an extended period of time as they accrue more things they need further storage space. Rather than having to buy a completely different storage system, a modular design allows them buy another unit of the same system and add it to the existing one. For the designer of such a system the key factor is how different individual units can be joined together. The connection is decisive. One famous example of this is the Haller modular furniture system from 1965. The design of the units is based on the architect Fritz Haller's original building for the Swiss metalwork manufacturer USM.[30] The building, completed in 1962, was designed so that as the company expanded the footprint of the factory could be extended simply by adding new sections to the modular steel frame. In 1963 Haller then designed a furniture system for the USM headquarters, based on the modular architectural design. Then in 1965 USM put Haller's system into production for the retail market. For such a system to be interchangeable and expandable the units had to be joined together and the parts needed to be standardized. USM then patented Haller's design for the joint, known as the ball joint or, more accurately, the 'heart-piece'.[31] The design meant that the framework for the units themselves could simply be screwed into the ball joints, and likewise the ball joints could be added across time as the system grew. The container corner fitting and Haller's ball joint: they are essentially the same type of device for joining things together. It may not be too farfetched to claim that the technical design of jointing systems has been at the forefront of architectural and engineering innovations. A further case in point is that of Konrad Wachsmann's work on the 'universal joint'.[32] Wachsmann, along with Walter Gropius, developed *The Packaged House* system in the early 1940s in the United States. The intention of the system was to apply mass-production fabrication technologies to architectural design, providing cheap and easily constructed housing. The basis for their approach was the use of a panel assembly system that could be flat-packed for ease of transport.[33] As with Haller's ball joint, and of course the container corner fitting, the key to the system was the way in which the panels could be joined together. This is where Wachsmann's design of the universal joint was decisive: the simple device enabled the panels to be locked together in a range of different configurations. For both jointing systems to be successful they have to be of a standard specification, and 'agreed-upon' size, so that in ten years' time the system can be extended.[34] The process can be repeated, almost ad infinitum. If we squint our eyes a little, a group of USM Haller units are not dissimilar to a stack of shipping containers. The premise for both is the same: through standardizing and regulating the specifications of the system the processes and procedures can be repeated. For architectural and design historian Reyner Banham such modular systems might, in theory, be said to be redolent of the mass-production processes of the early twentieth century, but he was also critical of whether standardization within architecture and design was actually any more than an aesthetic gimmick intended to simply *look* like a timeless solution. The argument in his famous 1955 essay, 'A Throw-Away Aesthetic', is reasonable: the purported timeless laws of an objective aesthetic are not to be found in a consumer product, particularly in the age of the throwaway aesthetic.[35] And although Banham's debunking of the purported Platonic ideal of standardization is charged with the fractiousness of the period, he also offers a constructive way of thinking about standardization in a broader sense.

Within the context of containerization, the role of standardization is even more complex than in architecture or industrial design, for it's an important example of standardization in practice. Although the container might possess the aesthetic of geometric simplicity, it is more than a symbolic gesture: it is a system at work. The long-drawn-out agreement over the standardized design and dimensions of the ISO intermodal container highlights how the regularization of the design specification ensured the container's compatibility and repetition of movement across the various transport networks. Standardization in the manufacturing process had been in existence since the rise of mechanization in the eighteenth century, and notably in relation to the use of *interchangeable* machine parts as well as in the manufacture of firearms.[36] The relationship to Haller's USM furniture system of interchangeable units is clearly evident. In the case of manufacturing processes, the standardization and interchangeability of parts was intended to eradicate any blockages in how various parts flowed throw a production line. Needing to constantly change parts, tailoring them to specific needs would inevitably hold everything up. The potential link between the automation of mass-production methods and the freight transport industry had already been raised by the first McKinsey & Co. report in 1966, when it argued that the technology to fully automate the freight industry had been available throughout the twentieth century. However the report went on to point out that one of the reasons for new technologies from mass-production manufacturing not being adopted was the power of the unions in resisting the move towards full automation due to the potential loss in labour, as was universally seen in numerous traditional port cities.[37] The history of mechanization and the later forms of standardization in manufacturing has a long and complex history: we could go back as early as the machines of the medieval period, through to the development of the printing press, but of course the most iconic mechanized process of all is that of the Ford Motor Company production line, developed by Ford in Highland Park in 1913.[38] That said, although the automobile has of course become the epitome of mass production and its attendant sociocultural impact, the role of mechanization reaches back to much earlier production processes, significantly the work of Oliver Evans and his mechanized grain mill from 1783.[39] Evans's design for the grain mill illustrates the overarching ideology of the assembly line: that of the 'speediest, most nearly frictionless transportation from each fabrication process to the next'.[40] Evans's production line offers a neat summary of the wider processes of mechanization and standardization: to promote continuous flow through the production process without interruption. The 'flow production' process, as initiated by Evans, provides an important backdrop both to later procedures developed by Ford, but also in relation to container handling as a similar form of purportedly near-frictionless flow. Of significant importance to the continuous flow of material in the early production line was the replacement of the human hand by the machine; the hand does not apparently have the rational logic of the machine. It became mechanized, just as the longshoreman's hook did. Whilst its ability to carry out various types of tasks are embodied in the mechanized actions of machinic systems such as Evans's grain mill, the hand, according to Siegfried Giedion, is incapable of one significant action: that of continuous activity and *repetition*.[41] The modus operandi of containerization is repetition of processes and actions; this can be seen at numerous container terminals around the globe – the same movements, the same systems for removing the containers from ships. For Andrew Barry the issue of repeated action is bound up with the use of standards (both material and procedural) to overcome potential problems in a particular system:

> The development of technology involves not just the reduction of blockages through the production of technical standards and other mechanisms, but the development of ways of circumventing or reconfiguring existing impediments.[42]

This is a valuable outline of the relationship between the role of standard procedures, standardized materials and the reduction in impediments to processes. This is still somewhat in the abstract: in the case of containerization the standardization of sizes and fittings, for instance, has to go hand in hand with *agreed* practices and procedures, such as the ways in which the technologies would be used. Looking back to the seemingly internecine discussions over container specifications, it was only once agreement between the parties was had that the universal application of the standards could be instituted. Added to this, through Barry's observations we might also think of standardization as a system with defined boundaries, or a closed system of sorts; by this I mean that the design of the standardized system of containerization facilitates the mobility of cargo through practices and procedures that are specific to freight cargo transport. For example, shipping containers can be connected to trains or trucks, but unless the corner fitting and twist lock are used this isn't possible. In theoretical terms this reading of standardization owes much to Michel Foucault's work on governmentality, whereby technological standards operate in a context 'which makes social domains knowable and governable'.[43] Such practices and procedures of governance are intrinsic to the development of global standards that allow institutional, corporate and governmental bodies to control various social processes, such as global commodity mobilities. Critically, as we'll observe in the next chapter, the 'beauty' of standardization and standards are that they facilitate 'at a distance' control over specific global processes, i.e., once standards are agreed upon they can, in effect, be trusted to work, albeit through continuous upkeep and management.

Before dealing with the globalization of containerization and its numerous effects, this final section considers in more detail how the design of the standardized system is constituted. Like Evans's grain mill, the system of containerization is based on the coordination of *connections,* in particular the relationship between all of the elements of the industry. This was where the earlier attempts at some form of unitized transport system failed. But crucially, as the container corner fitting demonstrates, there has to be a stabilization of relations, so that the connection between the container and the various modes of transport is 'guaranteed' through the universally recognized design. There has to be a *fit* between them – literally and conceptually.[44] The issue of guaranteed fit is an important one in the literature on standardization. The sociologists Geoffrey Bowker and Susan Leigh Star, in their work on classification, argue that standards are 'any set of agreed-upon rules for the production of (textual or material) objects'.[45] The development of the ISO container exemplifies this: only with the collective agreement on the standardized sizes could the design be fully implemented. There's another form of guarantee as well, and that is the one whereby the container itself is governed by internationally recognized standards, guaranteeing the regularity of design and its ability to interact with other standards such as the redesign of infrastructure. Through what might be called 'structures of agreement' standardization is the entrenchment of standards so that the various standardized parts of a system become 'crystallised' or solidified.[46] Through this process of entrenchment certain technologies and procedures are developed that help the standardized system to function. With containerization, the corner fitting and twist lock would be a case in point: it enables the interconnection with various transportation networks. This argument concerning standardization and interchangeability – or interconnection – speaks principally to the importance of stabilizing the moments of interconnection. And here we can turn to another sociologist to assist us with our 'interconnection of ideas'. Bruno Latour's work on the complexities of technological systems of various kinds offers a notable parallel to Siegfried Giedion's point about the repetitive qualities of the machinic as opposed to non-repetitive nature of the human hand. Latour talks of *delegation*. This is a process where human effort is delegated to socio-technical machines, be that a washing machine for cleaning clothes, a television remote control for enabling lethargy or, in Latour's example from the Introduction, an overhead door closer for assisting with operating a door. An object can be said to 'displace, translate, delegate, or shift' its function from one of major effort (such as opening a heavy door) to a minor one (displacing this into the light push of the door).[47] Through the design of the simple device of the container corner fitting, the previous work, effort and time expended on conjoining the container and vehicle (through the lashing of ropes) is built into the device: it is *delegated* to it. That is to say the purpose of this device (to link container and vehicle) replaces the previous job of the dockworker. In this sense the action of the worker is delegated to the corner fitting and twist-lock mechanism, albeit a mechanism that has to be locked in place by hand in certain cases. Critically, the expenditure of effort in lashing ropes around non-standardized containers is replaced by the 'dream of efficient action' embodied in the device itself.[48] This could be seen in another way: the technical know-how and skilled knowledge of stowage that longshoremen and stevedores previously practised and were paid for becomes delegated to the container – that is, unitization alleviates the craft of stowing cargo.[49] However, even with the delegation to technical objects, the process of stabilization is a relatively lengthy one, in that it takes time for a system of delegation to become entrenched or embedded, as seen with the previous discussion of the negotiations towards standardizing container design.

Inherent to all of these debates on the move to standardization is their politically charged nature: we saw this with the commercially driven struggles to agree on the standard sizing of containers, but we also saw – and still see of course – the way in which the mechanization and automation of freight transport profoundly changed the lives of those people whose skills and knowledge became redundant in the face of 'delegation'. As we'll now see, containerization was at the very heart of even larger-scale social, economic and geographical transformations at a global and, by implication, local level.

3 THE RISE OF THE WORLD-OBJECT

Hamburg SUG. Hapag-Lloyd. CMA CGM. Samskip.
Cosco. Maersk. Yang Ming. OCL. P&O Nedlloyd.
Evergreen. UASC. China Shipping. MSC.

These names should be much more familiar than they are. Although we might have spotted one or two of them on road or rail networks, given their centrality to the machinations of contemporary consumer capitalism it's surprising that they are not as ubiquitous as the Nikes, Apples or Starbucks of this world.[1] But as discussed in the Introduction this isn't quite so curious given the lack of focus on the distribution and circulation of commodities, particularly when compared to their production and consumption. These names are emblazoned on row upon row of containers at the Port of Rotterdam, the third largest container port in the world after Singapore and Shanghai. I am here on a boat tour of the port. The tourist vessel is well appointed with a restaurant and bar, populated today by groups of pre-Christmas revellers

FIGURE 4 Container ship being offloaded at Port of Rotterdam.

enjoying work celebrations. Aside from the work-related chatter they stare out blankly at the boxes – a little bored, by the look of their body language. Arms folded. A head propped up by a hand. Another head slightly drooped. To a certain extent this is understandable: just endless rows of containers, stacked on top of one another. There are a couple of others, like myself, who are on the external deck avidly photographing and filming these boxes and the infrastructural machinations that go on relentlessly. I film the elegant movement of the gargantuan gantry cranes as they lift the containers from the *Celina Star* with the automatic spreader bars that we heard about in the last chapter: the spreader bar lifter drops a container onto one of the waiting dockside vehicles. Even from the tourist boat you hear the clunk. Three to four seconds later the spreader disengages, rising up to pick the next container from the cells on the ship. It sways as it does so. Again you hear the clunk as the spreader engages with the container; another few seconds later it lifts it off. This takes just thirty seconds.

Rotterdam, like any other container port around the globe, is an incredibly complex machinic organism – one where over 1,000 people work, where some processes operate independently of one another, whilst at other times coming into contact. Human labour intersects with non-human entities such as the containers themselves, the computational infrastructure in the control rooms, bits of paper, emails, etc. All forms of social systems are made of enmeshed and overlapping interactions – Bruno Latour and Steve Woolgar told us this back in 1979 with their seminal study of the workings of a scientific laboratory.[2] Rotterdam demonstrates how much effort goes into maintaining this incredibly complex system, with the container at its beating heart. But Rotterdam also emphasizes how this system is *designed* to operate as efficiently as is feasible. Container ports work through flatness, vast swathes of endless horizontality. They are both the antithesis of urban verticality, and its offspring. In the drive towards the near total redesign of the infrastructure of freight transport that we began to consider in the previous chapter, two of the most significant effects were both the change to the geographical location of container ports and the design of ports themselves. Where the early images from *Men and Machines* depict scenes that could be from any time over the last few centuries, the latter ones can only be situated as twentieth-century phenomena. Looking to the work of Reyner Banham again, this time another characteristically prescient essay for *New Society* entitled 'Flatscape with Containers', he describes the move away from the traditional imagery of the port city with its 'craggy warehouses, masts, cranes and funnels silhouetted against the sky, picturesque Trotskyites in silk mufflers toting that box, lifting that bale, getting a little drunk'.[3] What it has moved to is radically different: 'What you see, more than anything else, is acreage of flat tarmac or concrete.'[4] Given the density of urban space, it is patently clear why the rapid development of containerization in the 1970s and 1980s resulted in the exit of maritime activities from classic urban centres such as London and New York. Whilst you can build higher with relative ease, it's nigh on impossible to construct vast expanses of flatness in central urban areas; it's expensive to say the least.[5] The point with containers and containerization is of course *speed* – this was clearly the fundamental rationale for the development of the system – a speed that comes with the levelling out of surface so that the container handling vehicles in the port, the trucks delivering and picking-up the containers can move as quickly as possible, and where the 'craggy warehouses' were the iconic buildings of maritime culture that disappears with containerization. There is no iconic architecture of containerization as such: the container is the architecture (a point we will consider in a little more depth in the Conclusion). Containers are mini, mobile warehouses if you like. The tall stacks of containers that loiter on the dockside are the closest there is to the magisterial buildings that Banham refers to, but soon they move on, loaded onto ships and sent off to the other side of the globe.

Even though containers may not potentially have the staying power of those dockside warehouse buildings that have become the homes of the financial classes since the 1980s, for some they have an elegance and logic of their own. Personally I find their geometric simplicity infinitely more pleasing than the nineteenth-century dockside warehouses. Banham rather wonderfully called this the 'goods-handling aesthetic of horizontal spread'.[6] And the very fact that Port of Rotterdam, like other container ports, is a tourist destination in its own right speaks to the somewhat mesmeric quality of these 'box parks'. This is about spectacle, both the marvel at the sheer scale of the port and the container stacks, and the concept of the 'spectacle' as the French writer Guy Debord described it: 'In societies where modern conditions of production prevail, all of life presents itself as an immense accumulation of *spectacles*. Everything that was directly lived has moved away into a representation.'[7] The shipping container is the image of contemporary capitalism. It is *the* representative object of capitalism. On a simple level it is used as the icon of present day capitalism: Benjamin Kunkel's book *Utopia or Bust* – a treatise on the crisis of capitalism – even has an illustration of a sinking container ship on its cover: the collapse of capitalism represented by the loss of commodities in containers.[8] Much in the same way that Debord describes the incessant, immanent presence of the spectacle in everyday life, so too the shipping container might be seen as an ever-present force in all that we do. To consume is to enter into the world of the container, although of course we only do so in retail outlets – we never see inside the container. As this chapter will argue, the rampant growth of consumer society is in part a result of the development of the shipping container and containerization. Although this is very much the case, one of the central reasons the ISO intermodal container has become so powerful an object of contemporary capitalism is precisely due to the fact that it moves so effortlessly without us noticing it. All we see is the blank face of the box.

Only when the apparent invisibility of these objects is punctured do we really begin to behold their true power. One case when this happened on a dramatic scale was on 18 January 2007. The container ship the *MSC Napoli* was making its way from Belgium to Portugal when it encountered gale-force winds and heavy seas off the south coast of England; fearing for their safety, the ship's captain ordered the twenty-six crew members to take to the lifeboats. The ship itself was once one of the largest container ships in the world with a capacity to hold over 4,000 containers, which by today's standards is relatively small. It was towed towards the English mainland, near Lyme Bay and the Port of Portland. However, there was a fear that the ship might break up, causing major environment damage, so the decision was made to take the vessel to the relatively calm and sheltered waters of Branscombe Bay, off the coast of Devon. This happened two days after the initial abandonment of the ship. Of the 2,318 containers that were on board, just over 110 of these were washed overboard. Fifty containers and their contents washed up on beaches along England's south coast over the next few days.[9] Most of them were on the beach at Branscombe Bay. Between 21 and 23 January large crowds gathered on the beach and began to salvage the contents of the smashed containers. The international media had a field day. There were wide-eyed reports that fixated on the kinds of things being scavenged: giant packs of nappies next to tins of dog-food; cans of spaghetti sat alongside packages of French perfume; grubby packs of shampoo; barrels floating in the sea; an upturned automobile lay damaged inside a shipping container; rolls of carpet; metal scrap; large rolls of plastic sheeting. One newspaper report described the scene as a marketplace, with people directing others to the specific location of goods strewn across the beach.[10] One image showed an overturned container with its contents strewn amongst the shingle, including a sofa, a lampshade, odd items of clothing: these were the belongings of a woman who was moving abroad, and using the container to transport her possessions – all now ditched on this beach. Another photograph depicted dozens upon dozens of people on the beach carrying their booty away, some with large barrels perched precariously on their shoulders, others wheeling them. Mangled containers dotted the beach, in an almost post-apocalyptic landscape. Most infamously, under cover of darkness a small group of scavengers were photographed manoeuvring an expensive BMW motorbike out of a container, their hoods raised but the faces still visible, with an understandable look of pleasure on them. Their stance is almost triumphal. The main report into the accident termed such activities a 'mendacious, national, and ultimately frightening interest in the prospect of illegal profit'.[11] But the desire of people to come to the beach and take what they found there was understandable. In part it speaks to an age-old mentality of subversion in the face of capitalism, but technically many of them were simply salvors. Under UK law the contents of the open containers were classified as salvageable goods, and governed by a twenty-eight-day rule whereby salvors have this time to report their finds to the Receiver of Wreck. However, if the containers were forcibly broken into, the beach would be deemed a 'crime scene': this happened on 24 January in an attempt by the police to reinstate order.

There is much to be learnt from this and other examples, most notably the story surrounding the 29,000 yellow plastic ducks washed overboard in a container in 1992 on a voyage across the Pacific from Hong Kong.[12] Not only have the floating 'Moby ducks' become a valuable tool for oceanographers studying oceanic currents, they also signal the nature of an ocean of commodities in circulation. As Donovan Hohn notes in his book on the lives of the ducks, hundreds if not thousands of containers are lost overboard on an annual basis, although little hard evidence is available as to the exact number. Even without this data to hand it's still an important illustration of the fact that so many containers and container ships are continually traversing the globe. According to latest figures there are nearly 6,000 container ships currently in operation with a capacity to carry almost twenty million containers.[13] These are truly *world-objects*. As we saw in the Introduction, the work of the French philosopher Michel Serres has focused on a number of different 'spatial characters', including the angels discussed previously. Back in the 1990s Serres described the ways in which bonds are created in both natural and social contexts, including examples such as agriculture where he describes a 'natural contract' between the farmer, the tools, and the land.[14] In a later essay entitled 'Revisiting *The Natural Contract*' Serres re-examined his earlier book, making it clearer still that such forms of 'contract' between people and the world around them were evermore urgent. In the essay he also offered a telling image of the power of another spatial character in mediating global spatialities – that of the 'world-object'.[15] Typified by 'objects' like telecommunication satellites and the Internet, these have the ability to produce the global age. They create the spatial and temporal relationships that we live by: 'We now live in those world-objects as we live in the world.'[16] I suggest that the shipping container is exactly this – an object that we live through. By this I mean that they are one of the paradigmatic objects of the global age.

In his discussion of Allan Sekula and Nöel Burch's striking film *The Forgotten Space* (2010), the Marxist geographer David Harvey describes how the movements of shipping containers suggest that it is possible to 'ride across the surface [of the ocean] in an unruffled way and bring the world into a unity of production and consumption'.[17] It strikes me that Harvey's rendering of containerization bears an important relationship to Banham's idea of the container 'flatscape': where the image of the container port as a space of expansive horizontality is extended onto a global scale. We might call this a 'global containerscape', where the globe is envisaged as a vast logistical surface of containers being moved in huge container ships before being moved onto rail and road networks. An apocalyptic version of globalization was the exact inference of the work of the Italian architectural collective Superstudio. In particular, their 1969 work 'Continuous Monument' depicts a gridded megastructure that engulfs the globe, reaching across vast swathes of urban centres and rural landscapes alike.[18] In perhaps the most iconic of the series we see one of these smooth, shiny mega structures surrounding the Manhattan skyline. Superstudio was offering a critique of the bland architectural and urban planning projects of the time. And although it was clearly a cultural critique, it was actually a very prescient description of the containerscapes of the present day. A British Telecom advertisement from back in 2005 shows a fictional cityscape where a container ship moves gracefully through the air alongside flows of parcels, gold bullion, gas cylinders, forklift trucks, people, security vehicles, rubbish bins, etc.; an IT specialist appears to choreograph the entire scene. Depending on one's reading of the advert this is a twenty-first-century version of 'Continuous Monument', the sci-fi-esque megastructure replaced by a megastructure of physical and informational flows. This also isn't too far from Michel Serres' idea of angels as medial things carrying messages through the ether. This isn't as fanciful an idea as it might first appear, for it is very much in keeping with the work of the anthropologist Arjun Appadurai who has discussed various forms of global '-scapes'. His five categories – ethnoscapes, mediascapes, technoscapes, financescapes, ideoscapes – all posit a picture of global flows of people, media, technology, money and political ideologies.[19] The containerscape of the BT advertisement is an amalgam of all these global-scapes.

These claims go some way towards highlighting Harvey's points about both the economic power of containerization and the important spatial aspect of globalization: that of the global *flows* of information, ideas and goods in particular, between sites of production and consumption. Within the geographies of contemporary capitalism, to raise the importance of the spatiality of flows is far from controversial. It's an obvious but valuable point of reference. And Manuel Castells' work on the space of flows posits the image of a world defined by movement, over and above an apparently static notion of place.[20] It remains a foundational body of work for discussions of mobility and the interconnectedness of global processes, including containerization. In the context of urban geographies Steve Graham argues that 'contemporary cities can be understood as socio-technical constructions supporting mobilities and flows to more or less distant elsewheres: flows of people, goods, services, information, capital, waste, water, meaning'.[21]

Extending beyond the hinterlands of the city, these flows of goods in particular define the power of the shipping container. But whilst the metaphor of flow points to a set of processes which identify the inherent mobility of capital, this has to be set against containerization's relationship with globalization. As we saw in the Introduction, for David Harvey containerization is 'one of the great innovations without which we would not have had globalization, [or] the deindustrialization of America'.[22] Although much debated, in overall terms globalizing processes can be said to have established a series of shifts, including the dominance of transnational capital where every country is integrated into a 'global production and financial system'.[23] As the BT advert implies, there is the growth of information, communication and transportation technologies. Culturally we see the development of a global class elite, as well as the growth of transnational political and economic systems, which are no longer necessarily linked to state-based forms of power. Inherent to this are the rise of new forms of insecurity, domination and inequality. This is of course a completely simplified depiction, and cannot in any way approach the complexity of contemporary global society. However, for the purpose of dealing with containerization the relationship between globalization and manufacturing is decisive. Crucially, at the heart of this relationship are increased flexibility in manufacturing processes, the shifts in traditional manufacturing bases from 'centre' to 'periphery'[24] and 'flexible' approaches to labour, including the loss of organized and unionized labour as well as the growing precarity of job security. In the context of consumer capitalism the move towards flexibility, in manufacturing processes in particular, underscores the interconnectivity of economic systems. Containerization has played a highly significant part in this system of global interconnectivity. For instance, we see a move from centralized forms of production processes under the wider auspice of Fordist mass-production technologies in 'core' countries, where '71 per cent of world manufacturing production was concentrated in just four countries and almost 90 per cent in only 11 countries',[25] towards the decentralization of production and the increasing manufacturing power of previously 'peripheral' economies. The development of the shipping container, in the post-Second World War context of the 1950s, tallies with the geopolitical aftershock of the war, where the manufacturing capacities of core countries other than the United States were destroyed. Alongside this, containerization is very much tied into the development of new industrial, communication and transportation technologies, including the growth of mass car ownership. However, for Peter Dicken the key factor was the growth of large-scale transnational corporations and their power to influence the role of governments through integrated trade, investment and macro-economic policy. The role of flexibility is again critical, for the power of these transnational corporations lies in their adaptability towards access to natural resources and raw materials, labour markets, capital and state subsidies. They didn't – and don't – need to be based in one country or even continent. Secondly, through their 'geographical flexibility' the corporations can move their resources and operations according to demand at national, international and global levels.[26] One significant manifestation of this change has been the rise of global production networks, where the interconnectedness of transnational corporations means that a range of different operations can be based around the globe – so that one element of a corporation's business, such as product development, can be situated on one continent whilst production is based in another. This is of course the face of global consumer capitalism.[27] The interconnected nature of such production mechanisms has an important bearing on the discussion of containerization and the wider field of logistics and supply chain management, of which containerization is a crucial element. Whilst a variety of production models continue to exist, including Fordist forms of mass production, for our purposes, one model in particular is significant for the rise of global container transport, and that is what Dicken terms 'transnational vertical integration'.[28] This is a rather complex system, but in a simplified form it essentially refers to a system where a range of raw materials, product components, semi-completed parts and finished items that a corporation produces are distributed around the globe according to their geographical location. Crucially, what this system of manufacturing demands is a much greater emphasis on two key factors: the importance of communication and transportation; the BT advert begins to make sense. Another significant factor in the globalization of manufacturing has been the rise of outsourcing. In effect outsourcing delegates aspects of one company's operations to another company. Primarily this happens when the external company has greater capability in producing a specific good or service (often more cheaply), leaving the main company to concentrate on their primary operations. Geographically, whilst outsourcing practices were initially contained within relatively close proximity, the advancements in communication and transport technologies (including containerization of course) have facilitated the use of outsourced suppliers from across the globe.[29] In this post-Fordist economy of outsourced, flexible production, geographical location plays an incredibly important role, but time is also a fundamental issue.

In post-Fordist economies the distributed nature of production and supply networks results in 'an obsessive concern with reducing the time in which goods are tied up unproductively either in inventory or waiting around for further processing'.[30] As noted above, if a corporation has various semi-finished components, raw materials and finished goods in different geographical regions it is imperative that their distribution and transportation is highly orchestrated. The shipping container's part in this should now begin to be clear: speed and efficiency of movement is vital. The technological and managerial platform most obviously associated with these spatio-temporal concerns is the 'just-in-time' system. As the name suggests, the key factor with this is the ability to transport components in order to provide them as and when they are required. This stands in stark contrast to the 'just-in-case' model associated with Fordism, where large stock inventories were held in order to provide a reliable supply of components. Here we can see the role of shipping containers as mobile mini-warehouses. Rather than components being stockpiled on one site taking up vast acres of warehousing, the shipping container is effectively a warehouse in transit. Allan Sekula and Nöel Burch sum this up rather nicely:

> As ships become more like buildings – the giant, floating warehouses of the 'just-in-time' system of distribution – factories begin to resemble ships, stealing away stealthily in the night, restlessly searching for ever cheaper labour. A garment factory in Los Angeles or Hong Kong closes; the work benches and sewing machines reappear in the suburbs of Guangzhou or Dacca. In the automobile industry, for example, the function of the ship is akin to that of conveyor systems within the old integrated car factory: parts span the world on their journey to the final assembly line.[31]

The key to such processes of just-in-time manufacturing is again the ability to keep the process *flowing*, so that 'parts and subassemblies must be transported to the producer/assembler relatively quickly and on short notice in order not to disrupt the flow of the production system within the assembly plant'.[32]

Flow is a strong spatio-temporal metaphor not only in the work of Manuel Castells, but also in the just-in-time system. Indeed the metaphor has been extended to describe these manufacturing processes as 'river-like', where the mouth of the river is the entrance to the market, and the processes prior to entrance to market are seen as the tributaries of the main flow of the river.[33] Such spatial and temporal metaphors are also an important facet of the shipping container's relationship with logistics and supply chain management. Put simply, the remit of commercial logistics is the control and management of the supply chain, enabling things to be moved in the most optimal fashion. For W. Bruce Allen logistics is

> a multidisciplinary approach concerned with how to coordinate all purchasing, selling, and producing activities together in order to assemble and distribute the right products in the right amounts to the right locations in the right condition so as to maximize profits for the firm.[34]

Of course this clearly bears on the discussion of just-in-time manufacturing and distribution, where the coordination of movement is imperative. What this suggests is how central transportation technologies have been to the development of global capitalism – if things are moving around the globe at an ever-increasing rate this has to be choreographed, all for the purpose of increasing profit. If logistics and supply chain management are now so embedded in contemporary life, this was not always the case. Up until the 1950s the role of transportation was seen simply as an inevitable fact of business activity, the assumption being that innovation was part of the product development and marketing processes; how to move things was deemed secondary. The rise of logistics and supply chain management in the latter half of the twentieth century is a complex story, involving the regulatory changes in transportation, including the US Shipping Act of 1984 that saw a move towards market-driven practices.[35] Coupled with this the potential value of transportation to corporate success came as a result of the recognized power of logistics in the Second World War and the Korean War.[36] The US recessions of the 1950s and 1970s, as well as oil embargoes, emphasized the potentially negative impact of rising transportation costs, inflation, interest rates and inventory charges. Whilst the 'logistics revolution' signalled the centrality of the physical distribution of raw materials and goods (aligned of course with containerization), logistics also encompasses storage and warehousing, the packaging of goods, informational systems, inventory and stock control, as well as transportation.[37] Where logistics primarily deals with aspects of supply, materials management and distribution, the supply chain extends beyond these domains. The concept of the supply chain began to emerge in the 1990s as it was recognized that logistical processes offered competitive advantage to companies, and that this could be broadened to encompass not only individual companies, but also a 'chain' of companies involved in all the various processes of product development for example.[38] So, where efficiencies had been premised on individual approaches, the supply chain model envisions a series of organizations linked by the supply chain itself, including producers, suppliers, distributors and retailers. Principally, supply chains emphasize the way in which the shift beyond the movement of commodities/raw materials broaches a wider organizational logic where the extended spatiality of corporate structures, necessitated partly by globalization, reaches beyond bounded national territories to encompass multinational corporate structures as well as extra-national allegiances.

All this is not to say that the rise of global supply chain networks or outsourcing came about as a direct result of the development of intermodal ISO containers from the 1970s onwards. Instead, what the shipping container and containerization help to flesh out are the profound structural changes that were instituted in the 1970s, 1980s and 1990s particularly in relation to manufacturing and distribution – changes that of course continue to this day. As a world-object the shipping container is very much part of an economic as well as spatial and temporal ideology that envisages the globe in a particular manner – one where it is imagined, partly metaphorically, as a smooth chain of movement, or as an efficiently operating diagram of sorts. However, as the next chapter will investigate, systems are inherently messy and require an awful lot of maintenance to function at all.

4 BREAKING THE SEAL

It's a grey, overcast and occasionally wet day. I'm in the passenger seat of a pickup truck at London Thamesport in the south-east of England. Despite its name London Thamesport is a container port situated some distance from any major urban areas, set on the River Medway. You need to drive some 50 miles to get into the heart of London itself. But the port is well connected to the rail and road networks on the outskirts of London, so it has become an important part of the United Kingdom's container infrastructure. Driving around the port I'm introduced to its various workings, including the dockside operations; the huge stacks of containers where they wait before either being loaded (usually empty) onto waiting container vessels, or more likely, given the flows of trade, offloaded before being picked up by trucks or trains; and the operations control room. The control room is interesting because although it's at the heart of the port operations it feels a little dishevelled: populated by soft drink cans, old coffee cups and other such remnants of human habitation. I suppose this is inevitable. Such an image stands in contrast to the automated container stacks where a model of efficiency appears to dominate. Given some of the discussions in the previous two chapters, the overall impression that you get from London Thamesport is the choreography of container movements, but this has to be protected – such levels of efficiency need constant maintenance. And I mean this in both senses of the word: through continual repairs to the technical infrastructure, and through its very safeguarding.

The security systems in place here testify to this. Only those truck drivers with the correct documents are granted entry into the port, where the use of encrypted data means that a driver must possess the correct reference number in order to be able to enter the port.[1] Once cleared to do so the driver is provided with a pager that identifies both the driver and the container they are there to either collect or offload, or both. This device is used by the driver to enter the main port through a security-gate system, at which point a dedicated printout provides the information about the location in the automated container stacks, where the container is either to be picked up or dropped off. Once this is carried out, for the drivers their allotted role within this port is ostensibly over with and they drive off using the pager to exit the system. On average this takes around thirty to thirty-five minutes. Devices like the pager system produce a secured system within the port that attempts, at least, to develop a structure based on the elimination of 'uncertainty', or more prosaically the refusal of entry to those individuals not cleared to enter. A further security feature at London Thamesport is the Customs clearance area. Here containers are weighed to check that their actual weight corresponds to the stated weight on the bills of lading. Likewise, containers that have goods of any animal origin are checked. The most striking device in this section of the port is the X-ray equipment: not dissimilar to a typical X-ray machine that one may have seen in a dental surgery, the X-ray scanner has a large boom that runs across the top of the container checking for any suspicious contents. These might include illegal arms or weapons, or more likely here at London Thamesport, smuggled tobacco or cigarettes.

The maverick philosopher Ivan Illich, reflecting on the fallout of industrial capitalist societies, argues persuasively that 'when an enterprise grows beyond a certain point on this scale, it frustrates the end for which it was originally designed, and then rapidly becomes a threat to society itself'.[2] This might be one way of considering the shipping container and containerization. It would not be overly dramatic to suggest that the container has been a colossal success, likely outweighing even Malcom McLean's initial plans in the 1950s. He's also unlikely to have thought that with the development of the ISO intermodal shipping container would come the potential threat to society that Illich imagines. Of course, Illich was not referring directly to the shipping container, but rather to the broader systems of industrial capitalism at that time. By contrast Gerald Mars in his striking book *Cheats at Work: An Anthropology of Workplace Crime* refers directly to containerization when he explores the relationship between organizational structures in workplace settings and the simultaneous ruses and forms of subterfuge created by employees to 'work the system', as he calls it. For him, new systems developed to alleviate workplace crime create further systems of subterfuge, from supermarket cashiers developing novel means of taking till money, through to containerization itself: 'The introduction of containers has reduced these opportunities [for theft], but it has increased others – not least because of what can be concealed in containers.'[3] So, those advocates of the move towards containerization, such as McKinsey & Co., did not perhaps envisage that all new systems are open to forms of disruption or disorder. With some twenty million shipping containers circulating the globe on an annual basis, it is perhaps unsurprising that they are co-opted and utilized for a range of illegal practices such as tobacco, cigarette and drug smuggling, but also for *people* trafficking and smuggling, along with potential use as 'weapons of mass destruction'. In similar ways to the so-called 'dark net', although the shipping container is the paradigmatic image of global capitalism it is also the engine of its own corruption.[4]

The shipping industry recognizes the potential threats from containerization and a number of initiatives were established in the post-9/11 world to deal with these. One, the International Ship & Port Facility Security Code (or ISPS), implemented in 2004 by the International Maritime

Organization, is intended to establish an international framework made up of national governments, governmental agencies, and the port and shipping industries, to develop preventative measures to alleviate threats to international trade. Whilst the International Maritime Organization is effectively the governing body for global shipping, the US government also set up a parallel initiative in 2006, the Container Security Initiative (CSI). The remit of the CSI is to protect the optimal trade routes that the flows of global goods require: it primarily is aimed at securing the supply chain. Crucially whilst the Initiative's aim is to counter any potential threats to the global movement of goods it also admits to its structural fallibility, noting the potential for shipping containers to be intercepted by criminal or terror organizations and enter US territorial space:

> To understand the extent of the U.S. security vulnerability growing out of international trade, it is important to understand the size and complexity of that trade. Since an estimated 95 percent of U.S. imports move by sea, the security environment must place a premium on detecting, identifying and tracking terrorist networks with interests in disrupting maritime commerce. ... Of over 100 million containers which moved through the maritime transport system in 2005, about 11 million arrived and were offloaded at domestic seaports in the United States, according to the Port Import Export Reporting Service (PIERS). The volume alone acts as a

significant enticement for a cargo container to be used as a conveyance for terrorism. Historically, containers have been used as a vehicle for the smuggling of contraband and human beings into the United States. The extension of these illegal activities into the realm of terrorism is a plausible but unacceptable outcome.[5]

This is a lengthy but telling statement. Although the sheer quantity of containers traversing the globe confirms the economic and political power of containerization, it also points to some of problems with knowing exactly where in the transport chain individual containers are and, crucially, exactly what they might contain.[6] One of the CSI's mandates is to pre-screen containers before they enter US territory, projecting the sovereign border of the United States beyond the territorial confines of the physical 'seam' of its mainland borders.[7] The strategy of moving the potential threat to US territory as far away as possible creates some interesting debates, not the least the geopolitical power of the United States to enforce this on trading partners. This isn't surprising of course. It also elicits debate on the very problem of interconnectedness that we discussed in Chapter 2. For one of the primary reasons shipping containers move so well is – once again – due to the fact that they are perceivably all identical and handled in the same manner the world over. To appreciate this is also to understand their *illicit* power.

Of course, you'll require a map to identify the location of the shipping container terminal itself, as well as the best point of entry. Before attempting to break into a container you need to enter the port by dressing as a dockworker: 'Dressed like this, you can enter Quai d'Atlantique without having any problems through one of the access gates after the lunch break, when you can intermingle with the other workers.'[8] Once safely into the port it's also possible to bribe one of the dockworkers if you have to. It's also necessary to obtain information about the date, time and destination of the container ships, often obtainable via publicized material. By this point, if you have managed to get into one of the containers it's imperative that you find where the air holes are located. Likewise you'll need to make sure you have a minimum of four litres of water, foodstuffs such as bread, meat, chocolate along with a flashlight and a few tools.

This is *Travel Guide*. However, it's not the familiar type of travel guide for the bourgeois cosmopolitan. This is an artwork by the Romanian artist, Matei Bejenaru. The work is witness to the ways in which the security mechanisms of containerization can be overturned. It also illustrates how the infrastructure of containerization is actually relatively simple to infiltrate. *Travel Guide* took the form of a foldout mock guidebook, and this particular version was presented in 2007 at Tate Modern in London as part of *The Irresistible Force* exhibition. Accompanying the text were a number of maps and photographs identifying points of entry, including the locations of shipping container terminals. It also consisted of a series of instructions and practical suggestions for travelling illicitly from Romania to the

United Kingdom or Ireland, including the drawbacks of travelling by bus from Romania, due to the fact that the majority of legal and illegal migrants travel by this means.[9] Whilst the French ports of Calais and Le Havre are deemed treacherous, given that the only practical means of crossing the English Channel is by stowing away in shipping containers or in the rear of roll-on-roll-off lorries, these are the primary sites for reaching the United Kingdom mainland. As the main 'vehicle' for travelling across the Channel, *Travel Guide* provides instructions on how to break into shipping containers, including a diagram showing the locking mechanism of the container doors.

Travel Guide is an incredibly potent means of dealing with the broader politics of how containerization and shipping containers have become the vehicle for what might be called 'smuggling logistics'.[10] Just as we saw above how commercial logistics and supply chain management practices are concerned with coordinating the movement of goods, so you could argue that illicit forms of logistics operate in a similar manner. Although such a claim might at first seem somewhat unsavoury the crucial point in this chapter is that containerization has brought about a number of unintended consequences. In effect the knowledge and practices that human-smuggling gangs or stowaways employ is an illicit form of logistical knowledge: rather than the management and control of legal forms of movement, these illegal actions are still about the way people or goods move.

And while examples such as *Travel Guide,* or series two of *The Wire* for that matter, demonstrate the cultural

Containers shipping in the ferry-boats in Le Havre

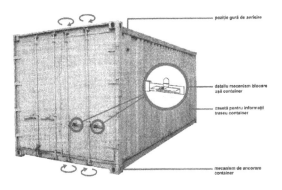

poziţie gură de aerisire

detaliu mecanism blocare uşă container

casetă pentru informaţii traseu container

mecanism de ancorare container

Locking mechanism of the containers

FIGURE 5 Container diagram from Matei Bejenaru's *Travel Guide*.

representation of smuggling in shipping containers, unfortunately numerous real life examples abound. On Tuesday, 4 December 2001, at the Port of Zeebrugge in Belgium, a people-smuggling gang moved thirteen Kurds into a supposedly sealed shipping container. The Kurds had made their way across Europe through different routes, each having paid approximately £5,000 to travel onto the United Kingdom.[11] Nine of the thirteen Kurds were to die through suffocation, a situation not dissimilar to the storyline in *The Wire*. Although much is made of the apparent efficiencies of containerization, in this case it was the *inefficiencies* of the system that led to a series of fatal errors. The journey from Zeebrugge to the Port of Dover in the United Kingdom should have taken eight hours but ended up taking five days. The container the group was stowed in was incorrectly picked from the container stacks at Zeebrugge and instead of being loaded onto a ship bound for the Port of Dover it was actually loaded onto a ship headed for the Port of Waterford in Ireland. On arrival at Waterford the automated stack system in operation (similar to the one in place at London Thamesport), with its lack of manpower present on the dockside, meant that the cries for help went unheard. There was then a further error: the container in which the group was stowed was scheduled to be loaded onto a truck, but once more the wrong container was loaded. It was only five days later – on Saturday, 8 December – that the group was eventually discovered, after being heard banging and screaming for help by a truck driver.

All too often it's as a result of such systemic errors that illegal migrants die in shipping containers. Incidents similar to the above include one in June 2000 where the bodies of fifty-eight Chinese citizens were discovered in a container at the Port of Dover. It appeared that the deaths were as a result of the refrigeration equipment being switched off and the doors locked shut.[12] Almost identical to this story were the deaths in a shipping container, due to a lack of ventilation, of fifty-four Burmese undocumented migrants seeking economic security in Thailand. The bodies were discovered after the driver of the truck stopped when the migrants banged on the container to alert him to the extreme conditions. More recently in August 2014 another story was reported by the UK media of the death of an Afghan man, Meet Singh Kapoor, who was found dead in a shipping container at the Port of Tilbury in the United Kingdom.[13] Like the case of the Kurds above, the container had been en route from Port of Zeebrugge with thirty-five Afghan citizens smuggled inside the container. After the eight-hour journey from Zeebrugge to Dover many of those inside were suffering from dehydration and hypothermia.

The differences between people smuggling, or human trafficking, and the smuggling of tobacco or illegal narcotics are all too clear in the examples above – the direct loss of life. But whilst these distinctions need to be borne in mind they do exhibit shared approaches to what the United Kingdom's National Crime Agency terms 'criminal logistics'.[14] The smuggling of illegal narcotics in shipping containers can be carried out through disguising them amongst more legitimate forms of cargo, in what is known as the load groupage. For example, in January 2012, again at the Port of Tilbury, UK Border Agency officers intercepted nearly two tonnes of cannabis smuggled into the United Kingdom from Cuba in a shipping container carrying a cargo of molasses that was stored in a tank.[15] The key point here is put well by the UK Border Agency itself: 'It is not unusual for smugglers to hi-jack perfectly innocent shipments in the hope they will evade detection.'[16] Another method, this time often used for smuggling tobacco, is to construct false floors that are built into containers allowing smugglers to hide tobacco in this hidden space.[17] The UK National Crime Agency has again stated that 'containerised freight is the main method used in the importation of [illegal] cigarettes'.[18] This was the case at London Thamesport where I was told that this particular method of adapting containers has resulted in an estimated fifty-two million cigarettes being smuggled in via London Thamesport between 2006 and 2007 alone.[19] If further proof were needed of the level of the trade in illegal and counterfeit tobacco, the UK government's HM Revenue & Customs agency has developed a strategy to tackle the distribution of such items. Since 2000 these strategies have included attempts to disrupt the supply chains of tobacco smuggling through increasing front-line staff, as well as the 'deployment of a national network of scanners to detect high volume smuggling in freight containers'.[20]

Of course, shipping containers are far from the only means of illicitly moving people or illegal goods around the globe.

There are also smaller-scale smuggling tactics, such as the use of yachts to smuggle cocaine from the Caribbean to the United Kingdom, under the legal guise of the yachting season. Alongside these are the more obvious use of drug mules in the form of personal couriers, and narcotics hidden in merchandise such as food tins, building materials or clothing.[21] But the factor that links these various methods of smuggling and the use of shipping containers is the dependency on harnessing established legal supply chains and transportation. And here the importance of the shipping container's intermodal nature comes to the fore once again. For the 'beauty' of the door-to-door-freight concept for smugglers is that once the illegal container enters the logistics pipeline it becomes almost invisible amidst all the others circumnavigating the globe. So although the design of the shipping container as a sealed unit means that it can be moved with much greater ease than break-bulk cargo, it also means that it offers the perfect space in which to conceal illegal practices. Of course, the vital question is: How are the containers themselves infiltrated?

In short, the answer is universality. The standardized nature of containerization in effect means that the procedures for moving these boxes are essentially the same the world over, as is the design of the container:

> Logically, a person who wanted to move dangerous things would watch the trade system in total, and look what gets caught moving through – what gets caught, how, when, and where. And look at what gets through: the simple

everyday commodities smuggled in the vast flow of trade. This, then, would probably seem a good way to move dangerous things.[22]

Travel Guide proves this. Standardization can backfire. Observation of the system highlights the potential areas of weakness: the areas where the fences are weaker, or the times of day such as lunch breaks where security might be reduced. In fact the International Maritime Organization recognizes this in its ISPS code when it notes the dangers posed by illicit observation of port facilities.[23] Where Gerald Mars calls this 'working the system', this might also be called 'knowing the system'. This type of internal knowledge is evidenced by the fact that hauliers or truck drivers are sometimes incriminated, both in the televisual world of *The Wire,* where some of the longshoremen were complicit in facilitating people trafficking, and the real world, where two truck drivers were charged with the murder of Meet Singh Kapoor. A further case in point is the misrepresentation of goods so that those listed on the Bill of Lading, or the container Manifest, are different to those in the container.[24] In this case the apparent legitimacy of the goods in containers, proven by the Bill of Lading and Customs clearance documentation, is used as a 'front' for the transport of more expensive loads, be that extra goods of the same type, or entirely different commodities altogether.

Crucially, it is the ability to conceal such practices that is paramount. As described earlier, the use of false floors in containers is intended to make the container appear absolutely normal, should it ever be opened by Customs or security officials. Evidence of tampering is decisive, particularly the attempts by smugglers to conceal evidence of interference with containers themselves. The tactics of infiltration primarily depend upon the security of container doors. The doors of containers have a metal plate welded to the right-hand door, which overlaps with the left door, keeping them shut. To secure the locking mechanism a seal is then placed through a hole in the lock of the right-hand door mechanism – this is intended to indicate whether or not the container locking mechanism has been tampered with during transportation. The seals themselves can take a variety of forms: almost domestic-looking cable ties; metal bolt seals; preformed metal seals which unravel if cut; seals with unique barcodes; through to electronic security seal devices. Radio-frequency identification (RFID) technology is an important and relatively recent addition to security seals. In particular it is claimed that active RFID seals can transmit information as to whether they have been removed, negating the need for visual inspections. Except for the latter, security seals aren't terribly effective. First, not all containers have to be sealed. In the context of the UK export system seals must be used only in the export of specific commodities such as bovine meat, cigarettes and alcoholic spirits. Secondly, legislation on the use of the seals themselves is far from standard. For instance, the system in the United Kingdom is rather convoluted. Here exporters need to use official HMRC seals, although under certain circumstances traders can use their own, but only ones that are officially sanctioned. The HMRC policy also provides guidelines on how to identify Customs seals, through identification marks such as the their official logo. Both the commercial seals and HMRC seals have unique serial numbers, as well as anti-tamper identifiers. Any evidence of breakage or illegal removal must be 'visible to the naked eye'.[25] Another potential fallibility in the use of container seals is the need to stop the official identification marks being copied. Fundamentally, in other situations the use of seals remains the choice of individual shippers, resulting in the situation where they are rarely employed at all.[26] Although the larger shipping lines such as MSC are now offering container-tracking services, this is not an industry-wide practice as yet. The anthropologist Carolyn Nordstrom describes a similar problem with identification through the use of the container numbering system. She points out just how simple it is to change a container's identity with some spray paint, scissors and paper stencil.[27] Although such wilful attempts to disguise a container exist, there are also more straightforward problems with mistaken identity: containers often have multiple identification numbers that have been accrued over a period of time and due to their palimpsest-like nature it's often difficult to ascertain which identification number is the correct one.[28] The role of the Customs seal or container identification number becomes decisive when some of the security procedures are considered. In particular, one of the most common practices for inspecting whether or not a container has been tampered with is a straightforward visual check. This will involve ascertaining that the seals have not been tampered with, then comparing the container information with the records. Whilst visual inspections are in evidence at ports such as London Thamesport, one industry agency identifies an important point about the problem of checking every container seal: unless 'its door locking mechanism and seals are checked at every interchange point, a tampered container is able to transverse interchange points undetected'.[29] Here you can see the trade-off between keeping all these boxes moving as quickly as possible and ensuring that they are also checked as regularly as is feasible.[30] Although the security rhetoric of the ISPS and CSI might suggest otherwise, for Nordstrom 'movement is primary, borders are secondary'.[31]

But even with visual checks the tactical ruses of smugglers are revealing. For the simple notion of a visual check doesn't necessarily take into account that the infiltration of containers can happen in such a way that the seals themselves don't *look* as if they have been disturbed and the doors broken open. In specific situations port terminal staff have been 'unaware that a container door could be opened without interfering with the seal'.[32] The two main methods of opening the right-hand door without noticeably damaging the seal are telling. First, the rivet that holds the door handle in place can be removed, which then means the handle can be lowered and the seal not damaged.[33] The left-hand door can then be opened after rotating the bar on the right-hand door. The second method of entry also involves removing the rivets to allow the seal to remain intact. The art of disguise is critical: when rivets are removed replacement ones can just be glued back on to hide the fact.[34] Related to this, one of the manufacturers of Customs seals notes on its website that the design of its metal strip seal is such that security inspectors are able to tell if it has been re-glued to conceal the fact that it's been tampered with.[35] We can appreciate then how the small-scale tactics of disguise, such as repainting the areas tampered with or gluing on fake rivets, suggest how the invisibility of individual shipping containers amidst all the others depends on an 'innocent' outward signification – not unlike nineteenth-century smuggling practices where tobacco was disguised to look like potatoes.[36]

These debates are telling for they offer an indication of the different scales of knowledge the container encompasses: on the one hand we saw how the logistics pipeline and global supply chains project an image of movement being managed within a bounded, secured space; whilst we then zoom into the granularity of gluing on a rivet to disguise the act of tampering. We might think of the first as a form of strategic knowledge, and the latter as tactical knowledge. Michel de Certeau's work on tactical knowledge is now an established reference for discussions of counterpoints to prevailing operations of strategic power that is associated with capitalism.[37] Although it may well be part of the intellectual canon it's still an incredibly valuable resource for investigating how power is utilized and turned against itself.

De Certeau's differentiation between strategy and tactics can almost be read as a model for this chapter, as he argues that unpredictability exists 'within [a] space ordered by the organizing techniques of systems'.[38] The operations of such managed forms of space are contrasted with the spaces of tactics, or what he calls 'the space of the other'.[39] Mirroring de Certeau's Lacanian predilections, the notion of the Other does not exclude the presence of this Other, rather it *requires* it. Central to tactical forms of knowledge and practice is the continued presence of strategic power, for tactics 'play *on* and *with* a terrain imposed on it and organized by the law of a foreign power'.[40] Tactical knowledge uses strategic forms of power to enact them for different ends. In effect the knowledge and practices that smuggling gangs, stowaways or contraband smugglers employ may be seen as an illicit form of logistical knowledge. Rather than logistics as the management and control of interconnection, this alternative form utilizes the self-same geographies of interconnection for illicit purposes.

To approach the idea of smuggling in shipping containers as a form of tactical knowledge also draws out an important debate about the very sanctity of global trade itself. Systems produce their own shadows. Capitalism does; so too with containerization. Legality and illegality are embedded in one another. And to return to the broader discussion of the relationship between production, distribution and consumption, distribution encompasses the legal and illegal. Jorge Dominguez suggests that smuggling is an inherently distributive practice, determined by various types of movement: from small-scale smuggling by individuals, through larger-scale operations such as weapons, to the 'under-invoicing' of goods declared.[41] As the latter point highlights, tobacco smuggling directly emerges from the imposition of import duties and taxes.[42] In historical terms, the legal and illegal movement of commodities occurred simultaneously, where in the eighteenth century for example smuggling was seen as central to both the circulation of labour and commodities.[43] Equally the development of free trade is said to run parallel to the contraband smuggling of this period. Indeed the forefather of the free market Adam Smith approved of smugglers as prototypical entrepreneurs[44] – a sentiment echoed by Gerald Mars when he describes the 'blurred line' between entrepreneurialism and fraudulent practices.[45] The point here is that it's impossible to disentangle the growth in sanctioned global commodity mobilities from the movement of illicit things, so much so that economic models of the free market can be seen to facilitate the removal of barriers to free trade movement as well as illicit trade.[46] There is then a crucial relationship – an entanglement if you want to put it that way – between existing flows of legal goods in shipping containers and the harnessing of these flows, where, 'hidden in the sheer volume of trade, in the economics of immediacy, in the logistics of transport, and in the contemporary revolutions in shipping lies the globalization of the illegal'.[47] This draws attention to the point that enmeshed in the parasitic harnessing of the 'economics of immediacy' and the logistical efficiencies of containerization, is the simple fact that the ISO shipping container is an incredibly convenient box in which to move things, be they legal or not.

CONCLUSION: CARGOTECTURE AND DISTRIBUTION FUTURES

The shipping container is a 'suitcase'.[1] This strikes me as an incredibly astute observation. I'm sitting on makeshift seating in the grounds of Godsbanen (a cultural centre) in the city of Aarhus, Denmark, talking to two people who run Institute for (X), a cultural and business platform for collaborative projects between artists, designers, musicians, craftspeople and entrepreneurs.[2] Dotted around us are approximately a dozen or so shipping containers that have been reconfigured into an array of different purposes – a bright orange one is emblazoned with the acronym 'U.S.E.' stencilled on the side, whilst on top a striking, large blue 'X' forms part of the logo for the Institute for (X). Its function is to store a wide range of equipment that is used for various cultural projects: an assortment of tools, bits of electrical equipment, all forming a mobile workshop. Just behind this sits another orange container, not quite so bright. This one is a little different as it is slotted into a wooden structure that extends out from one end of the container, and also above onto the top of the container. This strange, hybrid structure is a home, the container forming an integral part of the dwelling. It's almost the foundation for the home, a solid metal base for the wooden addition. Off to one side of this homestead sits another shipping container. Again a dwelling, this is older and a little more ramshackle, faded pale blue in colour with patches of rust dotted across its face. On the side of the container double-glazed windows and doors have been added, a slot cut into the metal to house them. It's quite shoddy, not unlike the one in *The Wire* where the longshoremen keep their office. Rather than the neat finish one associates with domestic double-glazing, here the meeting of metal and plastic frame is far from tidy. Expanding yellow foam oozes out from the gap where the two nestle together. This is not about the pristine finish of the domesticated environment – it's simply concerned with function: adding doors and windows that will keep this container dwelling a little warmer. The other containers here at Godsbanen form a similar range of purposes, some reconfigured into makeshift dwellings with doors and windows crafted from repurposed garden sheds. Others are more straightforwardly storage units for musicians and artists who work on the site. One neat, black 10-foot version has solar panels added to the top, providing sustainable energy to the music production studio housed inside. Like the opening example in the Introduction of the shipping containers at

Cove Park, their use here at Godsbanen is understandable. Why construct a workshop from scratch, for example, when you can simply buy one readymade, have it delivered, kit it out and use it immediately – particularly a workshop that needs to be moved about to a variety of locations? They make sense. The Institute for (X) is a constructive metaphor for the usefulness of the container itself. As a platform for whichever purpose it so chooses – effectively filling in the X – it can reconfigure itself accordingly. This is also very much the spirit of the organization that the institute forms a part of, Bureau Detours. The container is perhaps the thread that ties both together. Both the Institute and Bureau Detours have employed the shipping container on numerous projects. The stencilled acronym on the side of the bright orange container at Godsbanen reveals why: U.S.E. stands for 'Urban Space Expander'. It's a way of making space, of constructing environments for the exploration of new creative forms, or challenging prevailing ideas of how urban space is used. And whilst the allusion to Marx's notion of use-value is clearly present in the name, this is ultimately a rather more playful articulation of use-as-creativity. One of Bureau Detours' projects from September 2010, 'Free Furniture Factory', used U.S.E. as a mobile factory – located in the heart of Rotterdam – to produce furniture for people to take away free of charge and use around the city.[3] Another project in June 2013 that made use of U.S.E. was called 'USE Flotsam': this consisted of the U.S.E. shipping container being beached on the shoreline in the city of Aarhus.[4] The idea was ultimately to explore how washed-up flotsam in the form of old bits of wood, for example, could be used by people to make public space on the shoreline. Somewhat poignantly, on my trip to Aarhus a year later, this same shipping container still sits near the shoreline, the doors open, and smelling of urine. Whilst the notion of flotsam is something rather temporary in nature, and an important aspect of the shipping container more generally, a longer-term project by Bureau Detours is 'Container By' (or 'Container City'). This ongoing project, located along derelict railway sidings in Copenhagen, is looking to establish more permanent use of shipping containers to develop 'a platform for free-building experimentation and social entrepreneurship' including

FIGURE 6 U.S.E. shipping container at Godsbanen, Aarhus.

FIGURE 7 Container dwelling at Godsbanen, Aarhus.

workshops for producing music, and other production facilities for metal and wood.[5]

As noted at the end of the last chapter, shipping containers contain things, and they do this incredibly effectively. They can contain tanks of molasses, expensive German motorcycles, tins of food, alongside smuggled narcotics, tobacco and, all too sadly, people. But as the work of the Institute for (X) and Bureau Detours also suggests, the shipping container is a versatile piece of contemporary architecture due to its human scale, and ultimately a way of making space. For the idea of the shipping container being much like a suitcase is revealing. Outside of the context of containerized freight movement, the standard

ISO intermodal shipping container is quite simply a mobile box for storing things, as is a suitcase. They are also 'ready-mades' in the Duchampian tradition: already-existent objects that can be repurposed and reconfigured for different uses and different contexts. And part of the reason why so many containers have been repurposed for uses other than transporting cargo is precisely due to their versatility and flexibility. As far back as 1972 the architectural writers Charles Jencks and Nathan Silver recognized their potential: 'Obsolete shipping containers are being turned into quick prefab houses for disaster areas, the army in Vietnam and even ponies in the Netherlands.'[6] That they made such a comment in their book *Adhocism* is also quite revealing – for the shipping container might even be the perfect ad hoc object. Simply put, adhocism is a method of production that uses resources that are already available. Why expend energy and build something from scratch when perfectly acceptable and off-the-shelf objects and solutions are ready to hand? For example, if you require a receptacle in which to plant some strawberries it's not necessary to purchase a pot designed precisely for this purpose, particularly when you might have a perfectly acceptable water bottle that could be cut up and used. This is practically and economically sensible. Such everyday practices of adhocism attest to the way in which, as consumers, we intuitively reuse and reconfigure objects for practical purposes. As with the plant pot, this is often about the straightforward notion of a need being fulfilled. Rather than passive consumers, then,

Adhocism suggests that we are incredibly active in how we search out solutions to everyday problems, and in doing so we exhibit canny knowledge about the potentiality that objects have to become something other than what they were originally designed for. Jencks and Silver articulate how these acts of reformulation and transformation are both practical and political: 'The standardized and monotonous product is shifted from the repressive meanings often given it by corporations.'[7] That word *standardized* again, but here in a different context, for there is an interesting tension at the heart of the idea of the shipping container as an ad hoc object: one of the criticisms of the Modern Movement in *Adhocism* was the aridity of the uniform, standardized designs of the early twentieth century. That the shipping container is the paradigmatic object of standardization and uniformity seems like a curious reversal. But whilst it may indeed be an archetypal standardized, monotonous product, its meaning is not fixed by corporations. The activities of smugglers and Danish cultural collectives prove this. This also serves as a powerful reminder of the broader discussion of how objects always remain open to change. Things are not fixed; they evolve into new formations as they unfold over time. Utilizing Heidegger's concept of *phüsis*, the design theorist Cameron Tonkinwise notes, 'All things are in motion, especially those concrete everyday things which we moderns think are "at rest."'[8] Objects are always in a state of transformation, even though the finished state of mass-produced objects makes them appear as if they are static.

The container itself might be the perfect object to navigate this sense of continual change. For just as it was party to the radical changes to the fabric of urban life when many traditional maritime ports became redundant in the face of containerization, so too it has become an integral feature of the changing landscapes of urban life in the de-industrialized or post-industrial era. The rise of 'container urbanism' offers an interesting adjunct to the destruction of maritime port cities in the 1970s.[9] In London, for example, the Docklands area, devastated both by the move of the Port of London Authority out of the city itself, and Margaret Thatcher's policies of the 1980s, has seen innovative architectural experiments using shipping containers. The architects Urban Space Management – also responsible for the cargotecture at Cove Park – have been instrumental in the development of 'Container City' in Docklands in the early 2000s.[10] Similar to Bureau Detours' plans for their own 'Container City', the London site houses numerous activities such as office spaces, retail outlets, live/work spaces, artists' studios and community centres. For Urban Space Management the beauty of the shipping container as a piece of cargotecture is its versatility, cost effectiveness and the speed of assembly. The key point is that they can be linked together incredibly easily, just if they were being stacked in the cells of a container ship, or loaded onto the back of a truck. This level of speed and efficiency of architectural development mirrors the technical and structural innovations in the shipping industry, and accounts for the fact that hundreds of container architecture projects have been developed throughout the world, too numerous to mention here in detail.[11] Perhaps the most telling of these projects was the Dutch architectural practice MVRDV's un-built proposal for another 'Container City', this time to be located in Rotterdam. Constructed out of over 3,500 containers, the building looks as if it would have had a vast hangar-like quality, with shipping containers used for the walls, ceilings and floors. This scaled-up 'mega-container', some twelve containers high, 'creates a giant "bee-hive" with 3500 niches for sleeping, eating, exhibiting, and performing. It creates space for hotels, bars, galleries, a spa, conference spaces, shops, business units, ateliers, schools, and a crèche'.[12] The animation that accompanied the proposal for this mega container is a frightening, dystopian hell. Thousands of containers fly chaotically through the animated air before neatly slotting together to form a vast echo chamber, with the acoustic chill of 3,500 steel containers. The soundtrack is made up of sci-fi style garbled lyrics. Consumers relax in plunge pools cut into containers, others shop, some roam around looking at art, surrounded by Le Corbusier, Pierre Jeanneret and Charlotte Perriand's iconic LC4 chaise longues. As night descends 'Container City' is illuminated with pulsating strobe lighting. (It's not too different from the consumerist playground that is BOXPARK in East London.)[13] The fly-through descends into the cavernous main space with a huge fire pit in the middle. Given MVRDV's reputation for playful critique, perhaps this is capitalism in flames?

Depending on your ideological predilections, another dystopian (or utopian) future may be upon us in the form of additive manufacturing, more commonly known as 3D printing. This so-called 'third industrial age' has been said by some to be fostering in an era when consumers will be able to download files that can then be 'printed' three dimensionally on a domestic 3D desktop printer.[14] Although the likelihood of wide scale take-up of the technology is debatable there are potentially important changes to the production, distribution and consumption of material goods. In the context of manufacturing the very nature of mass production may be shifted. Where the rise of mass production was in part determined by increased economies of scale, the nature of 3D printing is such that individualized bespoke forms are possible, although at present the majority of applications are in the field of product prototyping.[15] There are potentially interesting changes afoot through the direct 'outsourcing' of production to the domestic space as opposed to the global south or China, for example.[16] This inevitably also has implications for the role of the consumer and the act of consumption itself. Although the conception of the consumer as a passive dupe has been challenged numerous times in the past,[17] with the potential to download and print bespoke artefacts on a domestic scale the role of the consumer as co-creator, or 'produser' becomes evident, if not necessarily inevitable.[18] Significantly the implications for distribution are perhaps the most telling. If consumers are able to print objects at home, or in relative close proximity to their homes in 3D printing hubs, then the very idea of global supply chains is put into focus. A recent article on this very subject of 3D printing and distribution has speculated that 'personal fabrication could mean that ships stacked with thousands of TEU containers filled with consumer goods become a remnant of the relatively recent past'.[19] Although the authors add that whether or not this will happen is totally unclear, their closing comments are a little more realistic: they suggest that certain elements of physical distribution are likely to remain alongside the development of these new platforms.

Also alongside 3D printing, the future of distribution is undergoing a significant amount of speculation at present. Perhaps unsurprisingly Amazon is at the forefront of some of this techno-utopianism through its development of drone delivery services and robotic warehouse pickers. The promotional video for its incipient Prime Air drone delivery service offers a sense of parcel delivery in the near future.[20] Initially the scene is quite familiar, one of Amazon's large 'fulfilment' centres with row upon row of consumer goods. One of these items is placed into an Amazon plastic box, not dissimilar to a child's lunch box – even the box clasp has that inane Amazon smirk logo. It is then sent on its way down a conveyor belt to be picked up by the waiting Prime Air drone. A couple of seconds later this lifts off and flies out of the warehouse, with that strange insect-like quality drones have. We then see it buzzing across fields at a relatively low height until it lands in the backyard of a house. It deposits its load before lifting off again, with the grinning householder all too eager to go fetch his order.

Another video, another Amazon 'fulfilment' centre.[21] This time there is an eerie silence to the scene, devoid of human presence. The only sound is that of the robots themselves. Around a dozen small orange Kiva Systems 'mobile robotic drive units' spin around before we see metal shelving units suddenly moving in an almost imperceptible manner: they seem to have an agency of their own. But the Kiva robots (each with their own number) are the ones lifting the shelving units from below. A 90-degree turn to the right, a swift 90-degree turn to the left – the robots move the shelves in that rectilinear fashion only automated systems can produce. This is nightmarish. Robots spinning, shelves moving, no human being in sight. This isn't the future: Kiva Systems robots are part of Amazon's eighth generation fulfilment centre programme where 15,000 of the robots are currently in operation.[22] This must have been what the impact of the shipping container was like for those longshoremen in the 1960s, faced with the spectre of automation and the loss of labour. They would likely agree with one description of this Amazon-world as a 'hyper-capitalist dystopia'.[23]

For others this is the future of logistics and distribution, a world devoid of human error, where the gentle hum of the Kiva robots is all that is heard. This is familiar territory of course. Even as the mechanization and automation of the shipping industry and cargo handling in particular alleviated some of the back-breaking labour of the longshoremen, its ultimate aim was to reduce the need for labour, coupled with reduced transportation costs and increased profit margins. But curiously, for all the deterministic posturing around how new generations of distribution robots and drone delivery services will supersede human labour, there is still the brute fact of the shipping container. Unless the economies of scale and the quality of production improves with 3D printing it is difficult to see a time in which commercial goods as well as raw materials will not need to be shipped around the globe. And still in these metal boxes – some of which rust; where the doors jam; the locks seize and the Customs seals are removed surreptitiously. But containerization does not stand still. As early as 1968 there were plans afoot for the development of container-carrying hovercrafts that could run on tracks and would be able to carry around twenty standard-sized containers at speeds of up to 150 mph.[24] Obviously, this never materialized. Container technologies do of course develop and there are numerous patents for improvements to the design of the container itself, including early designs from 1973 for a collapsible container, through to one from 2013 that proposed the use of a plastic polymer instead of steel as the main fabrication material.[25] The increase in the size of the container ships themselves has been the area where the most significant changes have occurred. Maersk's 'Triple E' class of ships, the first one of which came into service in 2013, is capable of carrying just over 18,000 containers. This number is the equivalent of a train of containers 68 miles long.[26] Although the figures are representative of the increasing importance of containerization as the dominant form of freight transport they also highlight potential changes to come, principally because their sheer scale is likely to impact on the importance of specific container ports that are large enough to handle these vast floating warehouses. With the launch of the first one in 2013 there were no North or South American ports capable of handling them, with China-Europe being the main route. But even with the technological advancements of these gargantuan ships the ISO intermodal shipping container still presents an almost lumpen face of contemporary capitalism. For, behind the apparent spectacular gloss of certain portrayals of consumer culture and the logistical might of immense container ships sits a metal box with packaged goods stuffed inside it.

LIST OF
ILLUSTRATIONS

ACKNOWLEDGEMENTS

As noted in the Introduction to this book, the shipping container has been of intellectual and creative curiosity to me since at least the early 1990s. The individuals whom I have discussed some of this fascination with are too numerous to mention in their entirety. However, many of the ideas in the book have been tested in a range of journal articles, including those published in *Mobilities*, *Environment and Planning A*, *Geopolitics*, *Tijdschrift voor economische en sociale geografie* and the *Journal of Transport Geography*, as well as book chapters in *Cargomobilities: Moving Materials in a Global Age*, *Architecture in the Space of Flows*, *Stillness in a Mobile World*, and *Nonsite to Celebration Park: Essays on Art and the Politics of Space*. I would like to thank the editors as well as others who influenced the work, including, Peter Adey, Anyaa Anim-Addo, Andrew Ballantyne, Thomas Birtchnell, David Bissell, Mat Coleman, Phil Crang, Isla Forsyth, Gillian Fuller, Steve Graham, Will Hasty, Alex Landrum, Eric Laurier, Hayden Lorimer, Peter Merriman, Kimberley Peters, James Robinson, Satya Savitzky, Chris L. Smith, Nigel Thrift, John Urry, Ed

Whittaker, and finally, Tim Cresswell in particular. I also thank Matei Bejenaru for his agreement to use images of his work, and Jette Sunesen at Godsbanen in Aarhus for putting me into contact with Institute for X, particularly Mads Peter Laursen. Likewise, thank you to Alexia Holt and her colleagues at Cove Park for permission to use the image in the Introduction. Finally, The University of Edinburgh has kindly funded aspects of this research.

NOTES

Introduction

1 See Kenneth Powell, 'Container Architecture', *Architects' Journal* 223 (May 25, 2006): 27–37.

2 See http://www.container-housing.co.uk (accessed 15 March 2015).

3 Intermodalism is defined as 'the use of at least two different modes of transport in an integrated manner in a door-to-door transport chain'. Organisation for Economic Co-operation and Development (OECD), *Intermodal Freight Transport: Institutional Aspects* (Paris: OECD Publications Service, 2001), 7.

4 Marc Levinson, *The Box: How the Shipping Container made the World Smaller and the World Economy Bigger* (Princeton, NJ: Princeton University Press, 2006), 171–88.

5 Mark E. Smith, Paul Hanley, Mark Riley and Craig Scanlon, 'The Container Drivers', *Grotesque (After the Gramme)* (Rough Trade Records, 1980).

6 See Daniel M. Bernhofen, Zouheir El-Sahli and Richard Kneller, 'Estimating the Effects of the Container Revolution on World Trade', *CESIFO Working Paper No.4136* (2013).

7 Benjamin Buchloh, David Harvey and Allan Sekula, 'Forgotten Spaces: Discussion Platform with Benjamin Buchloh, David Harvey, and Allan Sekula, at a screening of "The Forgotten Space" at The Cooper Union, May 2011', http://www.afterall. org/online/material-resistance-allan-sekula-s-forgotten-space (accessed 25 January 2012).

8 Mel Bochner, 'Serial Art, Systems, Solipsism', in *Minimal Art: A Critical Anthology*, edited by Gregory Battcock (Berkeley and Los Angeles: University of California Press, 1995), 92–102.

9 Allan Sekula, *Fish Story* (Düsseldorf: Richter Verlag, 1996).

10 See Levinson, *The Box*; Edna Bonacich and Jake B. Wilson, *Getting the Goods: Ports, Labour, and the Logistics Revolution* (Ithaca: Cornell University Press, 2008); Deborah Cowen, *The Deadly Life of Logistics: Mapping Violence in Global Trade* (Minneapolis: University of Minnesota Press, 2014); Rose George, *Deep Sea and Foreign Going: Inside Shipping, the Invisible Industry that Brings you 90% of Everything* (London: Portobello Books, 2013).

11 Siegfried Giedion, *Mechanization Takes Command: A Contribution to Anonymous History* (New York: W. W. Norton and Co., 1948).

12 Vilem Flusser, *The Shape of Things* (London: Reaktion Books, 1999), 45.

13 Flusser, *Shape of Things*, 19.

14 Ibid., 21.

15 Bruno Latour, 'Where are the Missing Masses? The Sociology of a Few Mundane Artifacts', in *Shaping Technology/Building Society: Studies in Sociotechnical Change*, edited by W. E. Bijker and J. Law (Cambridge, MA: MIT Press, 1992), 225–58.

16 Jesús García-Arca and José Carlos Prado Prado, 'Packaging design model from a supply chain approach', *Supply Chain Management: An International Journal* 13, 1 (2008): 375.

17 Henri Lefebvre, *The Production of Space* (Oxford: Blackwell, 1991), 340.

18 Lefebvre, *Production of Space*, 403.

19 Michel Serres, *Angels: A Modern Myth* (Paris: Flammarion, 1995), 8.

20 This relationship between angels and information is also explored by Peter Sloterdijk in his book *Bubbles*: 'Angelology is one of the historically indispensable means of access to the theory of the medial things.' Peter Sloterdijk, *Bubbles: Spheres I* (Cambridge, MA: MIT Press, 2011), 570.

21 Michel Serres, and Bruno Latour, *Conversations on Science, Culture and Time* (Ann Arbor: University of Michigan Press, 1995), 108.

22 Also see Nick Bingham and Nigel Thrift, 'Some New Instructions for Travellers: The Geography of Bruno Latour and Michel Serres', in *Thinking Space*, edited by Mike Crang and Nigel Thrift (London: Routledge, 2000), 281–301; Keller Easterling, *Enduring Innocence: Global Architecture and its Political Masquerades* (Cambridge, MA: MIT Press, 2005).

Chapter 1

1 Port of London Authority, *PLA Monthly* (May 1967): ix.

2 Ibid., xiii.

3 Port of London Authority, *PLA Monthly* (April 1974): 403.

4 Ibid., 393.

5 E. Schmeltzer and R. A. Peavy, 'Prospects and Problems of the Container Revolution', *The Transportation Law Journal* 2, 2 (1970): 263–99.

6 Louis Goldblatt and Otto Hagel, *Men and Machines: A Story about Longshoring on the West Coast Waterfront* (San Francisco, CA: International Londshoremen's and Warehousmen's Union, 1963).

7 See Donald Fitzgerald, *A History of Containerization in the California Maritime Industry: The Case of San Francisco* (unpublished PhD thesis, University of California, Santa Barbara, 1986): 5.

8 Giedion, *Mechanization Takes Command*, 5.

9 Goldblatt and Hagel, *Men and Machines*, 27.

10 No Author, Untitled Photograph. Neg. B8635, (Box 90.1, National Maritime Museum Photographic Archive, London, 1888).

11 Goldblatt and Hagel, *Men and Machines*, 30.

12 J. F. Kemp and P. Young, *Notes on Cargo Work* (London: Stanford Maritime, 1971), 50–1.

13 A. G. Ford, *Handling and Stowage of Cargo* (Scranton, PA: International Textbook Co., 1950), 205.

14 Goldblatt and Hagel, *Men and Machines*, 108.

15 See G. Van Den Burg, *Containerisation: A Modern Transport System* (London: Hutchinson, 1969), 24–31.

16 Van Den Burg, *Containerisation*, 23.

17 Ibid., 24.

18 Port of London Authority, 1967, xxvi.

19 McKinsey & Company, Inc., *Containerization: The Key to Low-Cost Transport* (London: McKinsey & Co., 1967).

20 McKinsey & Co., *Containerization*, 74.

21 Ibid., 75.

22 See Diana Twede, 'The Cask Age: The Technology and History of Wooden Barrels', *Packaging Technology and Science* 18 (2005): 253–64.

23 Miles Ogborn raises an interesting point concerning the shape and design of beer casks and barrels, both in terms of calibrating space, and in the role of collecting excise duty in the seventeenth century. Miles Ogborn, *Spaces of Modernity* (New York: Guildford Press, 1998), 171–85.

24 Ford, *Handling and Stowage*, 53.

25 Carl Knappett, Lambros Malafouris and Peter Tomkins, 'Ceramics (as Containers)', in *The Oxford Handbook of Material Culture Studies*, edited by Mary C. Beaudry and Dan Hicks (Oxford: Oxford University Press, 2010), 602.

26 Keith Harcourt and Thomas C. Cornillie, 'A Comparative International Study of Technology and Policy in the Development of Railway Freight Containerisation in the US & UK'. http://www.harcourt-consultancy.co.uk/Portals/3/KH-TN_Lisbon_Paper_Final.pdf (accessed 14 April 2015). I thank Peter Cox for this reference to work on early container designs in the context of railways.

27 Levinson, *The Box*, 29.

28 Van Den Burg, *Containerisation*, 150. Also see Fitzgerald, *History of Containerization*, 12.

29 Fitzgerald, *History of Containerization*, 13.

30 Levinson, *The Box*, 174.

31 No Author, *Link-Line Service Liverpool-Belfast* [Photograph] (Box 90.1, National Maritime Museum Photographic Archive, London, 1959).

32 H. E. Huntington, *Cargoes* (Garden City, NY: Doubleday and Co., 1964), 41.

33 Museum of Docklands, archive box 'Container Images' (loc.3.4), 'African Container Express, "Oil for shipment to Nigeria brought in by road transport in container at Tilbury Docks"' (1966, neg.2908-5).

34 Museum of Docklands, archive box, 'Container Images' (loc.3.4), 'Sealed container of Ford spare parts being loaded into *Waroonga*' (c.1960s. no negative number).

35 Museum of Docklands, archive box, 'Container Images' (loc.3.4): 'Gilbey's container in port being handled on the gauging ground at London Dock' (1965, neg.733167).

36 Berisford in,*Chitral* (no author), [Photograph] (Box 90.1, National Maritime Museum, Photographic Archive, London, 1967).

37 No author, *Chitral* [Photograph] (Box 90.1, National Maritime Museum Photographic Archive, London, 1967). The significance of the experiment is demonstrated by the fact that a reception was held on board the ship on 3 May 1967 to mark the event, with a board in the background stating 'P&O/ Berisford's Japanese canned salmon container experiment'. No Author, *Chitral*.

38 Frank Broeze, *The Globalization of the Oceans: Containerisation from the 1950s to the Present* (St. John's,

Newfoundland: International Maritime Economic History Association, 2002), 9.

39 W. Owen, 'Transportation and Technology', *The American Economic Review* 52, (1962): 410.

Chapter 2

1 Alexander Graham Bell, Aerial Vehicle, US Patent 757,012, filed 1 June 1903, and issued 12 April 1904. https://www.google.com/patents/US757012 (accessed 7 January 2015).

2 See Craig Martin, 'The Kissing Point', *N55 Book* (Copenhagen: Pork Salad Press, 2003), 382–7.

3 Schmeltzer and Peavy, 'Prospects and Problems', 263.

4 Ibid.

5 Broeze, *Globalization of the Oceans*, 9.

6 B. Gunston, 'Moving the Goods', *Design*, 234 (June 1968): 59.

7 McKinsey & Co., *Containerisation*, iv.

8 See Levinson, *The Box*, 36–53. However, Fitzgerald suggests that engineers such as Arthur Rohn had advocated for a complete overhaul of the freight transport industry in the 1940s, calling for the redesign of containers, ports, ships and the cargo handling equipment. Fitzgerald, *Containerization*, 6–7.

9 Levinson, *The Box*, 43.

10 Ibid., 47.

11 Broeze, *Globalization of the Oceans*, 31–2; Levinson, *The Box*, 53.

12 Levinson, *The Box*, 51.

13 Ibid.

14 Ibid.

15 Interestingly, there is variation in the date according to different sources. Van Den Burg states that one of McLean's unconverted T-2 vessels, the SS *Maxton*, sailed between New York and Houston on 20 April 1956. Van Den Burg, *Containerisation*, 154.

16 McKinsey & Co., *Containerization*, 6.

17 Marc Levinson notes that, 'loading loose cargo on a medium-size cargo ship cost $5.83 per ton in 1956. McLean's experts pegged the cost of loading the *Ideal-X* at 15.8 cents per ton.' Levinson, *The Box*, 52.

18 See Van Den Burg, *Containerisation*, 36–41. As Marc Levinson discusses, one of the other important factors in the adoption of the shipping container in the United States was the role they played in the Vietnam War. Prior to this the US Army had used a much smaller transhipment container called Conex boxes. But as with other early containers these were not as effective as the larger shipping containers. Further to this, Malcom McLean's company was also involved in developing the container-handling infrastructure in Vietnam to resolve the logistical problems that US military were facing with the use of Conex boxes. Levinson, *The Box*, 171–88.

19 Levinson, *The Box*, 148. For a discussion of the International Standards Organisation and their relationship with infrastructure more broadly, see Keller Easterling, *Extrastatecraft: The Power of Infrastructure Space* (London: Verso, 2014).

20 T. Egyedi, 'Infrastructure Flexibility Created by Standardized Gateways: The Cases of XML and the ISO Container', *Knowledge, Technology, & Policy* 14, 3 (2001): 49; Levinson, *The Box*, 137.

21 Schmeltzer and Peavy, 'Prospects and Problems', 264.

22 Van Den Burg, *Containerisation*, 41. Given this book was published before the final agreement on ISO sizing in 1970, there is a real sense of the tense struggle to find accord.

23 S. L. Falk, 'Introduction', in G. C. Thorpe, *Pure Logistics: The Science of War Preparation* (Washington, DC: National Defense University Press, 1986), xi–xxviii.

24 Easterling, *Extrastatecraft*.

25 Levinson, *The Box*, 51.

26 Jules G. Nagy and George W. Cooper, Universal Lifting Spreader, US Patent 3,458,229, filed 26 June 1967, and issued 29 July 1969, https://www.google.com/patents/US3458229?dq=3458229&hl=en&sa=X&ei=CElCVdyOJZbfauzqgKAI&ved=0CB4Q6AEwAA (accessed 3 December 2014).

27 Levinson, *The Box*, 142.

28 *Freeing Jammed Freight Containers and Container Fittings on Ships*, Docks Information Sheet No.1 (Revised), (Caerphilly: Health and Safety Executive, 2008).

29 Van Den Burg, *Containerisation*, 23.

30 Klaus Kemp, *The USM Haller Furniture System* (Frankfurt: Verlag Form, 1997).

31 Kemp, *The USM Haller Furniture System,* 19.

32 I thank my colleague Prof Remo Pedreschi for making me aware of Wachsmann's work on *The Packaged House System* and 'Universal Joint'.

33 For a study of *The Packaged House* see Gilbert Herbert, *The Dream of the Factory-made House: Walter Gropius and Konrad Wachsmann* (Cambridge, MA: MIT Press, 1984). Also see Alicia Imperiale, 'An American Wartime Dream: The Packaged

House System of Konrad Wachsmann and Walter Gropius',
Proceedings of ACSA Fall Conference (2012): 39–43; Pedro
Alonso, 'Diagrams of a Universal System of Construction in
the Work of Konrad Wachsmann: Between Representation
and Technology', *Proceedings of the Second International
Congress on Construction History* (Volume 1) (2006): 153–65.

34 As with much of the history of prefabricated, mass-produced
buildings, Wachsmann's and Gropius's Package House was
not a commercial success and Wachsmann left the production
company in 1949.

35 Reyner Banham, 'A Throw-Away Aesthetic', in *Design by
Choice*, edited by Penny Spark (London: Academy Editions,
1981), 90–3.

36 W. Higgins and K. T. Hallström, 'Standardization, Globalization
and Rationalities of Government', *Organization* 14, 5 (2007):
691; Manuel DeLanda, *War in the Age of Intelligent Machines*
(New York: Zone Books, 1991), 31.

37 McKinsey & Company, Inc., *Containerization – Its Trends,
Significance and Implications* (London: McKinsey & Co.,
1966), 5.

38 David Hounshell, *From the American System to Mass
Production, 1800–1932: The Development of Manufacturing
Technology in the United States* (Baltimore: Johns Hopkins
University Press, 1984), 10.

39 Giedion, *Mechanization Takes Command*, 79–86.

40 Ibid., 78. Following Hounshell's work, it should be noted
that there is no direct connection between Fordist methods
of the moving assembly line and Evans's 'flow production'
line. Henry Ford insisted that the main influence on his
standardized assembly line was the advancements in the
meatpacking industry.

41 Giedion, *Mechanization Takes Command*, 47.

42 Andrew Barry, *Political Machines: Governing a Technological Society* (London: Continuum, 2001), 18.

43 W. Higgins and W. Larner, 'Standards and Standardization as a Social Scientific Problem', in *Calculating the Social: Standards and the Reconfiguration of Governing*, edited by W. Higgins and W. Larner (Basingstoke: Palgrave MacMillan, 2010), 3–4.

44 Susan Leigh Star, 'Power, Technology and the Phenomenology of Conventions: On Being Allergic to Onions', in *A Sociology of Monsters: Essays on Power, Technology and Domination*, edited by John Law (London: Routledge, 1991), 26–56.

45 George C. Bowker and Susan Leigh Star, *Sorting Things Out: Classification and its Consequences* (Cambridge, MA: MIT Press, 2000), 13.

46 Egyedi, 'Infrastructure Flexibility', 41.

47 Latour, 'Where are the Missing Masses?', 229.

48 Ibid., 235.

49 It should be noted that the packing of containers still requires a knowledge of weight distribution, although this has itself been delegated to computer software packages such as CubeMaster (see http://www.logensolutions.com/VMS/CubeMaster/Cargo_Load_Plan_Optimization_Software_Overview.html accessed 23 March 2015).

Chapter 3

1 There is something of a subculture around 'container spotting' and infrastructure observation more generally. See Craig Cannon and Tim Hwang, *The Container Guide*

(San Francisco: Infrastructure Observatory Press, 2015), http://thecontainerguide.com (accessed 3 April 2015).

2   Bruno Latour and Steve Woolgar, *Laboratory Life: The Construction of Scientific Facts* (Princeton, NJ: Princeton University Press, 1986).

3   Reyner Banham, 'Flatscape with Containers', *New Society* 17 August (1967): 231.

4   Banham, 'Flatscape', 231.

5   Another important point about the location of container ports such as Rotterdam is that due to the size of the vessels the depth of the berths has to be much greater. With the scale of contemporary container ships, the depth needs to be at least 18 metres.

6   Banham, 'Flatscape', 232.

7   Guy Debord, *Society of the Spectacle* (Detroit: Black and Red Press, 1983), note 1.

8   Benjamin Kunkel, *Utopia or Bust* (London: Verso, 2014).

9   The main *Napoli* inquiry noted that one month after the beaching there were a total of 111 containers lost overboard, with fifty-eight on the beach at Branscombe, six washed ashore to the east of Branscombe, nine on the seabed and a further thirty-eight unaccounted for. As late as December 2008, the report states that 'industrial mop-heads like large sea urchins littered the beach' and that 'cargo will probably continue to be located ashore and on the sea bed of Lyme Bay for some years'. (Mercer 2009: 25). Ian Mercer, *MSC Napoli: The Aftermath of the Beaching off Branscombe, East Devon, 20 January 2007: Report of an Inquiry* (Exeter: Devon County Council, 2009).

10 Steven Morris, 'If you go down to the beach today … you're bound to find something to steal,' *The Guardian* (23 January, 2007): 3.

11 Mercer, *MSC Napoli*, 13.

12 Donovan Hohn, *Moby-Duck: The True Story of 28,800 Bath Toys Lost at Sea* (London: Union Books, 2012).

13 See http://www.alphaliner.com/top100/index.php (accessed 2 April 2015).

14 Michel Serres, *The Natural Contract* (Ann Arbor: University of Michigan Press, 1995).

15 Michel Serres, 'Revisiting *The Natural Contract*'. www.ctheory. net/articles.aspx?id=515 (accessed 3 January 2015).

16 Serres, 'Revisiting'.

17 Benjamin Buchloh, David Harvey and Allan Sekula, 'Forgotten Spaces'.

18 Peter Lang and William Menking, *Superstudio: Life Without Objects* (Milan: Skira, 2003).

19 Arjun Appadurai, *Modernity at Large: Cultural Dimensions of Globalization* (Minneapolis: University of Minnesota Press, 1996); also see Paula Bello, *Goodscapes: Global Design Processes* (Helsinki: University of Art and Design Helsinki Publications, 2008).

20 Mauel Castells, *The Rise of the Network Society* (Cambridge, MA: Blackwell, 1996).

21 Steve Graham, 'FlowCity: Networked Mobilities and the Contemporary Metropolis', *disP – The Planning Review* 144 (2001): 4.

22 Benjamin Buchloh, David Harvey and Allan Sekula, 'Forgotten Spaces'.

23 William I. Robinson, 'The Crisis of Global Capitalism: Cyclical, Structural, or Systemic?' in *The Great Credit Crash*, edited Martijn Konings (London: Verso, 2010), 290.

24 Peter Dicken, *Global Shift: Mapping the Changing Contours of the World Economy* (London: Sage, 2011), 14.

25 Dicken, *Global Shift*, 14.

26 Ibid., 61.

27 Ibid., 56.

28 Ibid., 140.

29 Ibid., 146.

30 Elizabeth Schoenberger, 'The Management of Time and Space', in *The Oxford Handbook of Economic Geography*, edited by G. L. Clark, M. S. Gertler and M. P. Feldman (Oxford: Oxford University Press, 2000), 324.

31 Allan Sekula and Noel Burch, 'The Forgotten Space: Notes for a Film', *New Left Review* 69 (May–June, 2011).

32 M. S. Gertler, 'The Limits to Flexibility: Comments on the post-Fordist Vision of Production and its Geography', *Transactions of the Institute of British Geographers* 13 (1998): 422.

33 M. Aoki, 'A New Paradigm of Work Organization: The Japanese Experience', *WIDER Working Papers 36* (1998): 13.

34 W. Bruce Allen, 'The Logistics Revolution and Transportation', *The ANNALS of the American Academy of Politics and Social Science* 553 (1997): 116.

35 For an invaluable critical study of contemporary logistics, see Cowen, *Deadly Life of Logistics*.

36 Allen, 'Logistics Revolution', 108.

37 A. Rushton, P. Croucher and P. Baker, *The Handbook of Logistics and Distribution Management [3rd Edition]* (London: Kogan Page, 2006), 7.

38 A. Rushton, P. Croucher and P. Baker, *The Handbook of Logistics and Distribution Management [2nd Edition]* (London: Kogan Page, 2000), 9.

Chapter 4

1 Author's field notes, London Thamesport (29 March 2007).

2 Ivan Illich, *Tools for Conviviality* (London: Calder and Boyars, 1973), x.

3 Gerald Mars, *Cheats at Work: An Anthropology of Workplace Crime* (Winchester, MA: Allen & Unwin, 1983), 6.

4 See Jamie Bartlett, *The Dark Net* (London: Windmill Books, 2015).

5 Office of Policy and Planning and Office of International Affairs, Container Security Division, *Container Security Initiative: 2006–2011 Strategic Plan* (Washington, DC: U.S. Customs and Border Protection, 2006): 11. For a comprehensive study of the security threats posed to global supply chains, and the role of the Container Security Initiative, see Cowen, *Deadly Life of Logistics*.

6 Although they are far from widespread in the containerized freight sector, RFID technologies are seen to be increasingly important in overcoming such problems. In particular, companies such as Savi Technology manufacture RFID sensor tags that can be affixed to a variety of containers. Larger container lines, including MSC, offer container-tracking services (see https://www.msc.com/gbr/help-centre/how-to-videos-1/tracking accessed 23 March 2015).

7   Deborah Cowen, 'A Geography of Logistics: Market Authority and the Security of Supply Chains', *Annals of the Association of American Geographers* 100, 3 (2010): 605.

8   Matei Bejenaru, *Travel Guide* (exhibited as part of *The Irresistible Force* exhibition, Tate Modern, 20 September to 25 November 2007): no page number.

9   The version presented at Tate Modern stated that as of 1 January 2007, when Romania joined the European Union, Romanians could travel freely to the United Kingdom and Ireland. Whilst this might be seen to reduce the potency of the project, it still highlights the struggle of other individuals to seek a new home for political or economic reasons.

10 A similar process of usurping legal logistics practice is evident in warfare, notably through 'insurgent logistics' (see M. E. Vlasak, 'The Paradox of Logistics in Insurgencies and Counterinsurgencies', *Military Review* (January to February 2007): 86–95.).

11 Paul Kelso, 'Chronicle of the Dover Tragedy', http://www.theguardian.com/uk/2001/apr/05/immigration.immigrationandpublicservices1 (accessed 4 January 2013).

12 W. Hoge, 'Bodies of 58 Asians in Dover: an "Evil Trade in People,"' *The New York Times*, 20 June 2000, http://www.nytimes.com/2000/06/20/world/bodies-of-58-asians-in-dover-an-evil-trade-in-people.html?pagewanted=1 (accessed 5 January 2006).

13 Jamie Doward, Meredith Thomas and Becca Harvey, 'Tilbury Migrant Death: "There were screams and then bangs on the door,"' http://www.theguardian.com/uk-news/2014/aug/16/tilbury-migrant-death-new-deal-zeebrugge (accessed 4 February 2015).

14 Serious Organised Crime Agency (SOCA), *The United Kingdom Threat Assessment Of Organised Crime* (London: Serious Organised Crime Agency, 2009–2010): 2.

15 UK Border Agency, '1.7 Tonnes of Cannabis Seized at Tilbury', http://www.ukba.homeoffice.gov.uk/sitecontent/newsarticles/2012/january/10-cannabis-tilbury (accessed 4 October 2013).

16 UK Border Agency, '1.7 Tonnes of Cannabis Seized at Tilbury'.

17 Carolyn Nordstrom, *Global Outlaws: Crime, Money and Power in the Contemporary World* (Berkeley: University of California Press, 2007), 129.

18 SOCA, *The United Kingdom Threat,* 18; also see Action on Smoking and Health (ASH), *Essential Information on Tobacco Smuggling* (London: ASH, 2010), 2.

19 Author's field notes, London Thamesport (29 March 2007).

20 HM Treasury/HM Revenue & Customs, *New Responses to New Challenges: Reinforcing the Tackling Tobacco Smuggling Strategy* (Norwich: HMSO, 2006): 8.

21 Manuel Castells, *End of Millennium: The Information Age – Economy, Society and Culture: Vol 3* (Oxford: Blackwell, 2000), 197.

22 Neffenger, in Nordstrom, *Global Outlaw*, 202.

23 International Maritime Organization (IMO), *International Ship & Port Facility Security Code and SOLAS Amendments 2002* (London: IMO, 2003): 78.

24 Nordstrom, *Global Outlaw*, 119–20.

25 HM Revenue & Customs, *Notice 205 Official Customs Seals and Trader Sealing (August 2011)* (Norwich: Crown Copyright, 2011): 8.

26 Nordstrom, *Global Outlaw*, 182.

27 Nordstrom, *Global Outlaw*, 185.

28 D. Mullen, 'The Application of RFID Technology in a Port', in *Port Technology International* (no date): 182.

29 M. Hawkins, 'Container Tampering', http://www.ukpandi.com/loss-prevention/signum-services/(accessed 27 January 2009).

30 Policy Research Corporation, *The Impact of 100% Scanning of U.S.-bound Containers on Maritime Transport (Final Report)* (Antwerp and Rotterdam: Policy Research Corporation, 2009): 45.

31 Nordstrom, *Global Outlaw*, 116.

32 M. Hawkins, 'Container Security', http://www.ukpandi.com/loss-prevention/signum-services/ (accessed 27 January 2009).

33 Hawkins, 'Container Tampering'.

34 Hawkins, 'Container Security'.

35 https://www.megafortris.co.uk/utility-seals/metalstrip-seals.html (accessed 15 April 2015).

36 Alfred Rive, 'A Short History of Tobacco Smuggling', *The Economic Journal/Economic History Supplement* 1, 4 (1929): 568.

37 Michel de Certeau, *The Practice of Everyday Life* (Berkeley: University of California Press, 1984).

38 De Certeau, *Practice of Everyday Life*, 34.

39 Ibid., 37.

40 Ibid. My emphasis.

41 Jorge Dominguez, 'Smuggling', *Foreign Policy* 20 (1975): 92; Nordstrom, *Global Outlaw*, 119–20.

42 M. Deflem and K. Henry-Turner, 'Smuggling', in *Encyclopedia of Criminology and Deviant Behaviour: Volume 2, Crime and Juvenile Delinquency*, edited by D. Luckenbill and D. L. Peck (Philadelphia: Brunner-Routledge, 2001), 473.

43 Marcus Rediker, *Between the Devil and the Deep Blue Sea: Merchant Seamen, Pirates, and the Anglo-American Maritime World, 1700–1750* (Cambridge: Cambridge University Press, 1987), 72.

44 Deflem and Henry-Turner, 'Smuggling', 473.

45 Mars, *Cheats at Work*, 49.

46 Gargi Bhattacharyya, *Traffick: The Illicit Movement of People and Things* (London: Pluto Press, 2005), 33.

47 Nordstrom, *Global Outlaw*, 158.

Conclusion

1 Author interview with Mads Peter Laursen from Institute for (X), 30 June 2014.

2 http://detours.biz/projects/institut-for-x/ (accessed 3 March 2015).

3 http://detours.biz/projects/free-furniture-factory (accessed 3 March 2015).

4 http://detours.biz/projects/use-flotsam/ (accessed 3 March 2015).

5 http://detours.biz/projects/container-by/; and http://cargocollective.com/containerby/ (accessed 3 March 2015).

6 Charles Jencks and Nathan Silver, *Adhocism: The Case for Improvisation* [expanded and updated edition] (Cambridge, MA: MIT Press, 2013), 70.

7 Jencks and Nathan Silver, *Adhocism,* 68.

8 Cameron Tonkinwise, 'Is Design Finished? Dematerialisation and Changing Things', in *Design Philosophy Papers: Collection Two*, edited by A. M. Willis (Ravensbourne: Team D/E/S Publications, 2005), 23.

9 Mitchell Schwarzer, 'The Emergence of Container Urbanism', *Places Journal*, February (2013), https://placesjournal.org/article/the-emergence-of-container-urbanism/ (accessed 3 February 2015).

10 http://www.containercity.com (accessed 3 February 2015).

11 See H. Slawik, J. Bergmann, M. Buchmeier and S. Tinney, *Container Atlas: A Practical Guide to Container Architecture* (Berlin: Gestalten, 2010).

12 https://www.youtube.com/watch?v=3h_xqLWeIVo (accessed 30 March 2015).

13 BOXPARK, in the Shoreditch area of east London, is a 'pop-up' shopping mall constructed out of refitted shipping containers. See http://boxpark.co.uk (accessed 15 July 2015).

14 Chris Anderson, *Makers: The New Industrial Revolution* (London: Random House, 2013).

15 Victor Buchli, 'The Prototype: Presencing the Immaterial', *Visual Communication* 9, 3 (2010): 273–86.

16 *The Economist*, '3D Printing: The Shape of Things to Come', www.economist.com/node/21541382 (accessed 4 January 2012).

17 Alvin Toffler, *The Third Wave* (New York: Bantam Books, 1981).

18 S. E. Bird, 'Are We All Produsers Now? Convergence and Media Audience Practices', *Cultural Studies* 25, 4–5 (2011): 502.

19 Thomas Birtchnell and John Urry, 'Fabricating Futures and the Movement of Objects', *Mobilities* 8, 3 (2013): 402.

20 http://www.amazon.com/b?node=8037720011 (accessed 23 February 2015).

21 https://vimeo.com/113374910 (accessed 23 February 2015).

22 http://www.designboom.com/technology/amazon-kiva-robots-generation-fulfillment-12-02-2014/ (accessed 6 January 2015).

23 John Lanchester, 'The Robots are Coming', *London Review of Books* 37, 5 (5 March 2015): 8.

24 R. Stanton-Jones, 'The Future Development of Hovercraft: The 1968 Lord Sempill Paper', *Production Engineer* 47, 8 (1969): 365–83; also see Van Den Burg, *Containerisation*, 151.

25 Patent US 3,765,556/US 2013/0233755: A. Baer, Collapsible Shipping Container, US Patent 3,765,556, filed 11 September 1969, and issued 16 October 1973, http://www.google.co.uk/patents/US3765556 (accessed 12 March 2015); Frederick Lampe, Transportation Shipping Container, US Patent 2013/0233755, filed 7 March 2012, and issued 12 September 2013, https://www.google.co.uk/patents/US20130233755?dq=patent+2013/0233755&hl=en&sa=X&ei=3GBDVarUJtavabr-gagE&ved=0CCEQ6AEwAA (accessed 12 March 2015).

26 R. Neate, 'Giants of the Sea Force Ports to Grow', *The Guardian* (7 March 2013): 33.

INDEX

Page references for illustrations appear in *italics*.